Hero Myths & Legends of
Britain & Ireland

HERO MYTHS & LEGENDS

OF BRITAIN & IRELAND

M. I. EBBUTT

EDITED AND INTRODUCED BY

John Matthews

With new illustrations by

PETER KOMARNYCKYJ

BROCKHAMPTON PRESS

LONDON

A BLANDFORD BOOK

First published in the UK 1995 by Blandford
An imprint of Cassell plc
Wellington House, 125 Strand
London WC2R 0BB

This edition published 1998 by Brockhampton Press,
a member of Hodder Headline PLC Group

ISBN 1 86019 8716

Edited from material in *Hero Myths and Legends of the British
Race* by E. I. Ebbutt and published in the UK in 1910

**A Cataloguing-in-Publication Data entry for this title is
available from the British Library**

Typeset by Keystroke, Jacaranda Lodge, Wolverhampton

Printed at Oriental Press, Dubai, U.A.E.

Contents

Editor's Note   vii

INTRODUCTION: The Timeless Realms   1
The Dream of Maxen Wledig   11
Havelok the Dane   20
Cuchulain, the Champion of Ireland   36
The Tale of Gamelyn   52
Black Colin of Loch Awe   68
The Marriage of Sir Gawain   82
King Horn   98
Robin Hood   118
Hereward the Wake   134
Further Reading   148

Index   150

Editor's Note

In selecting nine stories from the 1910 edition of M. I. Ebbutt's famous work, it will be apparent that modern considerations have necessitated a title change from the original *Hero-Myths and Legends of the British Race*.

A further point of note is that while a modern typeface has been adopted for the resetting of the selected stories, the original spellings of names have been retained in order to keep the flavour of the 1910 edition, even though some of these will be considered outdated and inaccurate. This should be acknowledged in any further reading on the subject.

For a similar reason, some selected original illustrations are reproduced, along with the new colour plates which have been specially painted for this edition by Peter Komarnyckyj.

The selected stories have been provided with brief introductory essays by John Matthews, which are intended to provide a context for the tales, with relevant historical, legendary and mythological backgrounds. Inevitably, the diverse origins of many of Ebbutt's stories, their varying content and information available have determined the scope and emphasis of each of these specially written introductions.

The Timeless Realms

We remake our mythology in every age out of our own needs. We may use ideas lying around loose from a previous system or systems as part of the fabric. The human situation doesn't radically alter and therefore certain myths are constantly reappearing.

The Erotic World of Faery by Maureen Duffy

AROUND the turn of the nineteenth century, a number of books appeared which have since become minor classics within their genre. All dealt with the native traditions of Britain, Ireland, Scotland and Wales and with their myths and legends. They included *Celtic Myth and Legend: Poetry and Romance* by Charles Squire; *Romance and Legend of Chivalry* by A. R. Hope Moncrieff, and *Myths and Legends of the Celtic Race* by T. W. Rolleston, published in 1911 and 1912. All were characterized by a wide knowledge of the subject, coupled with a sympathy towards the people and times described, and a sensitivity towards the language of the original works which resulted in good and generally accurate versions. At a time when translations from the Celtic languages were still few and far between – and scholarship lagged even further behind – these books were indispensable tools for the interested reader, as well as being gateways into the timeless realms of the native myths and stories of the British Isles.

This newly edited edition of *Hero-Myths and Legends of the British Isles*, as it was originally titled, is another such volume as those listed above. It, too, set out to give an account of the many cultural elements that had gone into the making of the mythology of Britain: Celts, Romans, Saxons, Danes, and Normans – all had influenced the development of the country's racial character, and hence its myths.

It was from books such as these that the children of the early twentieth century first learnt of the rich heritage of mythology. Some of the attitudes expressed in Ebbutt's versions may well strike us as old-fashioned and even nationalistic, and this is perhaps inevitable in view of the time when the book was written, when the British Empire (itself soon to become something of a myth) still flourished. However, the author's avowed statement that he sought 'to come as close as possible to the Medieval mind' is still true, and we should not be too quick to attribute Edwardian values to what may in fact be far older.

When Ebbutt was working on *Hero Myths and Legends*, the era of Empire was waning. Mighty Britannia, which was actually composed of numerous peoples drawn to her shores, was beginning to decline. The power balance of Europe was in serious trouble, despite the wide-seeding descendants of Queen Victoria and her Albert. Even as Ebbutt was finishing this book, the First World War loomed on the horizon.

But the men who went to fight in the Great War of 1914–18 did not go wholly unprepared for heroism. Behind them, actively part of their heritage, were such stories as are represented in this collection. Those who died at Passchendaele and on the Somme were reared from the cradle upwards on the heroic epic poem: Lord Macaulay's 'Horatius', Lord Tennyson's 'The Charge of the Light Brigade' and Lord Byron's 'The Destruction of Sennacherib' were the character-forming stuff of Victorian and Edwardian life.

The collection fails to take into account the rising tide of feminist consciousness that was abroad when Ebbutt was writing. The female suffrage movement, which sought to gain the vote for adult women and remove them from the powerless limbo which they shared with criminals, prisoners, and the insane, was equally inspired by stories of female heroism. The acts and exploits of heroic women were often featured in the many pageants and dramatic tableaux which were being staged at this time: the resistance of the warrior queen Boudicca against the Romans, the canny wisdom of Elizabeth I, and the heroic vision of Joan of Arc, yet to be canonized, were the no-nonsense, unambiguous heroines in their own right who appeared most often in these dramas.

Of native heroines, Ebbutt makes no mention. For him, the role of hero was very much a male one: a concept that reflects his sex and upbringing, since the conception of female heroism was both alien and unnerving at this time. Ironically, it was the very act of war and the many heroic and unsung deaths which brought about a limited female suffrage, causing the social and mythic role of women to be radically revised.

Ebbutt's original selection contained several more tales, some of which are either less interesting to modern readers or are so readily available as to make their inclusion here unnecessary. In selecting the nine tales which make up this edition I have tried to choose the best and more representative of the subject – those 'hero myths and legends' which reflect the varying natures of the peoples who gave them life. Thus you will find Celtic ('The Dream of Maxen Wledig', 'Cuchulain, the Champion of Ireland'), Saxon ('Hereward the Wake' and 'Robin Hood'), Scottish ('Black Colin of Loch Awe'), Arthurian ('The Marriage of Sir Gawain'), and those which can only be called English ('Havelok', 'King Horn', and 'The Tale of Gamelyn') and within these, references to Norman and Danish characters.

The Hero

Heroes are hard to define and probably every age has its own ideas of what names a man or woman heroic. As the writer Rosemary Sutcliff put it in her book *Heroes and History* (London: Batsford, 1965):

> It is hard to know, still harder to tell, what makes the Hero, though when you find him, you know him instantly and beyond doubt. Being a great man, a great leader, someone supremely good and brave and wise, doesn't make a Hero; indeed, though he *may* be all these things, and is always a great man in one way or another, he very often is not particularly wise or good. But he has something about him that other men haven't got. . . . He has a special kind of magnetism that lives on after him, so that stories gather to him, even other men's stories, or tales that were old before he was born. He wears, like Cuchulain the Champion of Ulster, 'The hero-light on his brow'.

Such are the people whose deeds and adventures are to be found within this book. Every one possesses that special quality, the 'hero-light' which had drawn the heroes of stories from other ages and heroes into its ambience.

Though there is no such thing as the archetypal hero, several attempts have been made to define the common aspects which go to make up figures such as those to be met with here. Probably the best known is Sir George Frazer's huge multi-volume study *The Golden Bough* (1935) though this is bewildering to most readers in its sheer size. An equally interesting and informative book is *The Hero* by Lord Raglan (1936). In this the author attempted to codify the aspects by which the typical hero could be recognized. These are as follows:

1 The hero's mother is a royal virgin.
2 His father is a king, and
3 Often a near relative of his mother, but
4 The circumstances of his conception are unusual, and
5 He is also reputed to be the son of a god.
6 At birth an attempt is made, usually by his father or his maternal grandfather, to kill him, but

   7 He is spirited away, and
   8 Reared by foster parents in a far country.
   9 We are told nothing of his childhood, but
  10 On reaching manhood he returns, or goes, to his future kingdom.
  11 After a victory over the king and/or a giant, dragon, or wild beast,
  12 He marries a princess, often the daughter of his predecessor, and
  13 Becomes king.
  14 For a time he reigns uneventfully, and
  15 Prescribes laws, but
  16 Later he loses favour with the gods and/or his subjects, and
  17 Is driven from the throne or city, after which
  18 He meets with a mysterious death,
  19 Often at the top of a hill.
  20 His children, if any, do not succeed him.
  21 His body is not buried, but nevertheless
  22 He has one or more holy sepulchres.

Whether these are the only, or even the most typical, characteristics of the hero I leave the readers of this book to decide for themselves. Certainly a number of the aspects listed above are present in the stories which follow, as you will see as you read on.

Heroes come into being for a number of reasons. Sometimes they emerge from history – like King Arthur, or Robin Hood, or even Hereward – because the time needs them. Sometimes they are recognized as heroes by certain specific acts, as in the case of Gawain, Colin of Loch Awe, or Gamelyn. Above all they represent a certain standard – of bravery, honesty, even a kind of innocence. They face the world in a way that is all their own – unaffected by the fashions or mores of the time; driven, often, by a need to discover their own limitations, or to put right the wrongs they perceive around them. They may, like the Arthurian Knight of the Round Table, swear an oath:

> Never to do outrage or murder, always to flee treason; also, by no means to be cruel, but to give mercy unto him that asketh mercy, upon pain of forfeiture of their worship and lordship of King Arthur for evermore; and always to do ladies, damosels and gentlewomen succour, upon pain of death. Also, that no man take up a battle in a wrongful quarrel for no law, nor for no world's goods.

At other times the hero is driven and instructed by no single goal, no particular sense of duty or binding rule, but rather by an instinctual grasp of what is required by the period, the circumstances, or the moment. All the heroes have one thing in common – they act in such a way that they bring about huge changes in the lives of those around them – whether by redressing some great wrong, as in the case of Robin Hood, or by simply following an inner vision, like the Emperor Maxen in the opening story who travels across half the world to find the woman he has seen only in a dream.

The Nation's Dream

To a large extent heroes express national pride and character, and it has been truly said that one can tell more about the character of a people from the heroes they choose than from almost any other source. As the folklorist Christina Hole wrote in her book *English Folk Heroes*:

> Every nation has its real or mythical heroes, whose deeds are chronicled in song, ballad and story and whose legends form part of the national heritage of history and folk-lore. Such legends are . . . frequently founded, at least in part, upon fact; they are full of stirring incidents [and] . . . are connected with places well known to their hearers and with people whose names have long been household words. They enshrine the most cherished traditions of the race to which they belong, and are handed down from generation to generation as proof of what the race could once do and may in the future do again.

Which goes to show that it is neither by the literature nor the history of a people that national identity is formed, but by its myths. In the British Isles so many great heroes have come and gone that it is hard to find one who is more representative than another. The two figures who stand at opposite poles, who represent originally opposing cultures but whose nature and function are essentially the same, are Arthur and Robin Hood. Arthur is probably the closest thing we have to a national hero, and Robin Hood, who not only connects us to a very distant past but is also a perennially current hero, stands as guardian and protector of the outcast.

Arthur's origins go back into the mists of time, perhaps to an ancient Celtic bear god, yet it is as the heroic leader of men that he claims his place in British folklore, the warrior leading other warriors at a time when invaders from across the sea threatened to overrun the country. Appearing at this time of great need, Arthur welded together the disparate factions among the Celtic tribespeople and made them into a force which pushed the Saxons, Angles and Jutes back to our shores and re-established a central government when chaos reigned on every side. Though he probably lived for no more than forty years, his name became a symbol of native resistance which kept it alive down the ages. Long after his passing, when his enemies, the Saxons, had made England their own, stories of this great hero, taken across the narrow sea to Gaul by fugitive Britons, returned on a new wave of conquest, as the Normans, under the leadership of Duke William of Normandy, in turn overcame the Saxon people. Stories of Arthur, now a 'king', became the favourite subject of countless romances and songs, until the ancient Celtic warrior was the most famous hero of the Western world.

This fame was further distilled by the widespread myth that Arthur *was not dead*, but lay sleeping in the realms of Avalon – or under a variety of hills in different localities – ready to re-emerge when the times and needs of the land required his help. Arthur, like the earlier Celtic hero Bran the Blessed, takes on semi-immortal status in his guardianship of the land, acting as a palladium and protector long after his withdrawal from the affairs of serial time.

Ironically, it was the oppression of the Saxons by the Normans that brought Robin Hood to the fore. As a representative of the last dying flicker of opposition by the 'native' people of England, he stood forth as a beacon of the poor folk against the harsh tyranny of the newcomers. Just as Arthur was a courtly hero, beloved of knights and squires, lords and ladies alike, whose deeds are centred upon the individual adventures of nobly born men and women, so Robin, in the shape of the Green Man whose human representative he was, was connected irrevocably to the land and, through the image of the greenwood, to an ancient lineage of folk tradition which predated both that of Arthur and his own manifestation as the Outlaw of Sherwood.

Interestingly, in the fourteenth-century poem 'The Little Gest of Robin Hood', the outlaws swear an oath not unlike that of Arthur's knights – showing once again how close the bonds of hero with hero truly are, despite the separation of time and culture:

> Look you do no husband harm,
> That tilleth with his plough;
> No more you shall on good yeoman,
> That walked in greenwood shawe;
> Nor no knight nor squire
> That would be a good fellow . . .

Heroes and the Land

Heroes are remembered by the land that gave them birth. In the British Isles there are literally thousands of places whose names recall heroes both known and unknown. Places such as Wayland Wood in Norfolk, which remembers the mighty smith god of the Saxons; or Pendragon Castle in Cumbria which recalls Uther Pendragon, father of King Arthur; or Dinas Bran in Wales, which is named after the Celtic god Bran. Literally dozens of stones, cromlechs, hills and caves are named after Arthur himself – bearing a silent testimony to the sheer power of the legends of Britain's greatest hero.

In Ireland, there were so many stories which tied story to place that a vast book, *The Dindsenchas*, was compiled in the Middle Ages, listing thousands of places with their associative myths or stories. Many of these have since been forgotten but the names linger on in places: for instance that of the River

Shannon, named after the goddess Sinann; Meath, named for the Druid Mide; the Boyne River, which recalls the goddess Boand; and the Plain of Mag Murcraime (the Plain of Pig-numbering), so called because of a story in which a herd of magical swine was once caught and counted there.

Not surprisingly, in view of the number of sites which have their own local legend or folklore, the stories retold here are often set in specific places, many of them still recognizable. We may still walk in Sherwood Forest (or in the Forest of Barnsdale in Yorkshire where Robin Hood is also sometimes found), or visit the Isle of Ely where Hereward kept the Norman soldiery at bay. Grimsby in Lincolnshire, where Havelok's adventures began; Loch Awe where the descendants of Black Colin still live; the mound of Emain Macha, where Cuchulain drove his mighty chariot pulled by two magical horses – all are there to be seen and explored.

When overseas visitors come to Britain, it is not to see the factories, office blocks and housing estates of the modern era: they come to commune with the land and its history, to be inspired by the landscape which is threaded through with a multi-stranded web of story with which local people are continually in touch at a deep level. The Greek philosopher Heraclitus taught that 'you can't step into the same river twice' and, indeed, the impossibility of visiting the past *as it was at any previous era of history* is one of the great frustrations of visitors who have read the stories and recreated the landscape of Britain in their imaginations. Historical interpretation centres which seek to reproduce or give a flavour of past centuries and ways of life are ultimately unsatisfactory because the imagination can picture these scenes much more colourfully and vividly.

The Tale-Bearers

One of the most wonderful things about many of these stories is the way they mutate, changing names and places, mixing and remixing themes with each successive telling, while yet never losing their central focus. E. K. Chambers, in his book *The English Folk-Play* (Oxford: Clarendon Press, 1933), recalls the story of a horseman leaping off Bedrugan Head in Cornwall to escape pursuers. This story, Chambers tells us, was once told of Tristan, later of Sir Bors, and finally of one Henry of Bedrugan, who fought on the wrong side at the Battle of Bosworth. 'The lapse of folk-memory,' he adds, 'is as characteristic as its tenacity. When I passed Athelny last year, a Glastonbury car driver called my attention to a farmhouse where "Arthur" burned the cakes.'

It is to the tale-tellers that we have to look for such marvellous tricks of time and place. The deeds of heroes are remembered wherever people gather to hear the old tales told over again. In our own time the art of storytelling is undergoing an astonishing renaissance, with individual storytellers and larger organizations springing up everywhere.

In the Middle Ages, where most of the stories in this book first sprang to life, wandering tale-bearers, called *conteurs*, took the adventures of Arthur and his Knights, of the Paladins of Charlemagne, of the Nine Christian Worthies, to every part of the land. Earlier, scalds, professional tale-weavers of the Northern peoples, recounted their own great hero tales, locating many of these in the land where they had chosen to settle. Earlier still, the bards, the professional storytellers of the Celts, wove their own magic into the web of story through cycles such as the Irish 'Tales of the Red Branch Heroes' of which Cuchulain was the foremost hero; or, in Wales, the series of Wonder Tales collected into the four great books which make up *The Mabinogion*.

How many of these stories have not survived we can never know – lists of tales from both Irish and Welsh tradition suggest that there were many more which were never written down, and which perished as they were gradually forgotten. Fortunately, enough of them did survive to give us a rich heritage of lore and wisdom which comes directly from the many peoples which have gone into the making of the modern English race.

Even as Ebbutt was writing his book, another great English writer, G. K. Chesterton, published a poem called 'The Myth of Arthur' which in fact says a good deal about the nature of the hero and the way he is perceived. It seems a fitting way to end this brief introduction:

> O learned man who never learned to learn,
> Save to deduce, by timid steps and small,
> From towering smoke that fire can never burn
> And from tall tales that men were never tall.
> Say, have you thought what manner of man it is
> Of whom men say 'He could strike giants down'?
> Or what strong memories over time's abyss
> Bore up the pomp of Camelot and the crown.
> And why one banner all the background fills,
> Beyond the pageants of so many spears,
> And by what witchery in the western hills
> A throne stands empty for a thousand years.
> Who hold, unheeding this immense impact,
> Immortal story for a mortal sin;
> Lest human fable touch historic fact,
> Chase myths like moths, and fight them with a pin.
> Take comfort; rest – there needs not this ado.
> You shall not be a myth, I promise you.

*

C. I. Ebbutt's 'hero myths' still provide a good introduction to the native mythology of the British Isles. It is hoped that the selection which follows will encourage readers to look deeper into the heritage of these legend-laden islands and, to this purpose, brief lists of further reading relevant to each story can be found at the end of the book. To give an idea of the original texts from which these stories are drawn, I have included in my introduction short extracts from more or less contemporary sources.

JOHN MATTHEWS
Oxford

The Dream of Maxen Wledig

THIS story originally appeared in the great collection of Welsh folk myth and saga first published in English from 1838 to 1849 under the title *The Mabinogion*. Edited and translated by Lady Charlotte Guest, it included tales written down during the Middle Ages but containing the remains of far older material, dating from the sixth to ninth centuries. Celtic scholarship was only about sixty years old when Ebbutt was writing, and the publication of Guest's translation of *The Mabinogion* brought popular attention to the literature of the Welsh peoples for the first time in England.

The Maxen Wledig of the title is, in all probability, the Emperor Magnus Clemens Maximus, whose career can be summarized as follows. He served with Theodosius in Britain, earning fame both as a leader and as a fearless fighter. At the time the Roman Empire was in its death throes and ruled over by several emperors. Maximus, a popular leader, was proclaimed Emperor by his own troops in AD 384 and departed for Gaul with the intention of taking control of Rome itself. He was met in the field by the Gratian, the Emperor of the West, whom he defeated. Helped by his old comrade Theodosius, who had by this time become Emperor of the East, Maximus successfully occupied Rome in AD 388. However, his reign was short-lived, as he fell out with Theodosius, who had him murdered.

In the following story Maxen marries Elen, the daughter of Udaf (or, as she is called here, Helena). However, though this may well be a memory of Maximus having married a British wife, the story is only half true. In reality it represents both an ancient traditional theme and a folk memory of another emperor, and indeed records something of Britain's relationship with Rome itself.

Elen, or Helena, is in actuality a conflation of two people. Helena, the wife of Constantius Chlorus, was probably the daughter of the Brythonic king Cole of Colchester (the Old King Cole of the nursery rhyme) and is herself the mother of Constantine the Great, the first emperor officially to recognize Christianity. Helena's influence on his decision to do so resulted in her being canonized as St Helena, and a number of apocryphal stories sprang up around her – including the claim that she discovered the relic of the Cross used in the crucifixion of Jesus.

On to this already complex history is grafted a mixture of folk tales and memories concerning Elen, also known as Elen Lluddog, Elen of the Hosts (the Legions?). She is remembered as the builder of a series of paved roads connecting the Roman fortress of Segontium (modern Caernarvon) with the rest of Wales and England. Local tradition refers to these roads by the name *Sarnau Elen*, or Elen's Roads. These were in all probability ancient trackways improved by the Romans at the behest of Constantius Chlorus, and their ascription to the actions of the Emperor's wife probably derives from her confusion with a more ancient, tutelary deity of the area, whose roads were sacred paths connecting ritual sites.

The fact that in the original story Elen is also described as one of the 'Daughters of Branwen' marks her out as a goddess of the land, a representative of Sovereignty, with whom the ruler of the country must mate or marry in order to be in a harmonious relationship with the earth. The fact that this more ancient Elen has been conflated with the Roman Helena illustrates the uneasy relationship which existed between the invading Romans and the native Britons. Though there was never a true peace or accord between the two, the benefits – in the shape of improved roads, better living conditions, and a more or less stable monetary system – were often appreciated by the native peoples who, despite their conquered status, adopted the ways of Rome in many areas of Britain.

Maxen's dream falls into the category of the *aisling* (visionary dream) of which there are numerous examples within Celtic (especially Irish) tradition. In most cases these involve the appearance, in dream, of an other-worldly woman, frequently representing the Sovereignty of the Land, who leads the king, or hero, on a voyage into or across the land over which he rules or whose king he represents. Maxen, dreaming of Elen, is led on a journey which takes him across the western half of the Empire to Britain, then to Wales and specifically to Segontium or Caer Seint where he finds the woman of his dream and marries her. The symbolism of the voyage, the journey and the description of the hall where he finds her, are all drawn from the rich traditions describing the Celtic Otherworld. Maxen, in journeying there, and in subsequently marrying Elen, is in fact establishing a contract with the land – symbolically representing the contract between Rome and Britain seen after

The dream of the Emperor

the event as a spiritual union of the two countries. Whether it was ever viewed in this way during the occupation of Britain is an intriguing thought, though one for which there is no precise evidence.

It is possible also that the story recalls a now-lost tale in which Julius Caesar, having dreamt of the British maiden Fflur (flower), stole her away to Rome. In this context we can see that once again this was a representation of the Sovereignty of the Land, and there are tantalizing references in the ancient Welsh *Triads* to the British king Caswallawn (the historical British king Cassivellaunus) having pursued Fflur to Rome disguised as a shoemaker, and of his having rescued her – in this way winning back his stolen sovereignty.

Thus what on the surface seems a simple and charming story has a far deeper meaning and becomes one of the central tales depicting the inner history of Britain.

Though Lady Guest's version of *The Mabinogion* has been several times superseded by more recent translations, no one has succeeded so well in capturing the rhythms and nuances of the original. The following extract gives a good idea of this, in the description of what Maxen sees in his vision as he arrives at the castle over the sea:

> . . . the gate of the castle was open, and he went into the castle. And in the castle he saw a fair hall, of which the roof seemed to be all of gold, the walls of the hall seemed to be entirely of glittering precious gems, the doors all seemed to be of gold. Golden seats he saw in the hall, and silver tables. And on a seat opposite to him he saw two auburn haired youths playing at chess. He saw a silver board for the chess, and golden pieces thereon. The garments of the youths were of jet black satin, and chaplets of ruddy gold bound their hair, whereon were sparkling jewels of great price, rubies, and gems, alternately with imperial stones. Buskins of new Cordovan leather on their feet, fastened by slides of red gold.
>
> And beside a pillar in the hall he saw a hoary-headed man, in a chair of ivory, with the figures of two eagles of ruddy gold thereon. Bracelets of gold were upon his arms, and many rings were on his hands, and a golden torque about his neck; and his hair was bound with a golden diadem. He was of powerful aspect. A chess-board of gold was before him, and a rod of gold, and a steel file in his hand. And he was carving out chess-men.

The Emperor Maxen Wledig

The Emperor Maxen Wledig was the most powerful occupant of the throne of the Caesars who had ever ruled Europe from the City of the Seven Hills. He was the most handsome man in his dominions, tall and strong and skilled in all manly exercises; withal he was gracious and friendly to all his vassals and tributary kings, so that he was universally beloved. One day he announced his wish to go hunting, and was accompanied on his expedition down the Tiber valley by thirty-two vassal kings, with whom he enjoyed the sport heartily. At noon the heat was intense, they were far from Rome, and all were weary. The emperor proposed a halt, and they dismounted to take rest. Maxen lay down to sleep with his head on a shield, and soldiers and attendants stood around making a shelter for him from the sun's rays by a roof of shields hung on their spears. Thus he fell into a sleep so deep that none dared to awake him. Hours passed by, and still he slumbered, and still his whole retinue waited impatiently for his awakening. At length, when the evening shadows began to lie long and black on the ground, their impatience found vent in little restless movements of hounds chafing in their leashes, of spears clashing, of shields dropping from the weariness of their holders, and horses neighing and prancing; and then Maxen Wledig awoke suddenly with a start. 'Ah, why did you arouse me?' he asked sadly. 'Lord, your dinner hour is long past – did you not know?' they said. He shook his head mournfully, but said no word, and, mounting his horse, turned it and rode in unbroken silence back to Rome, with his head sunk on his breast. Behind him rode in dismay his retinue of kings and tributaries, who knew nothing of the cause of his sorrowful mood.

The Emperor's Malady

From that day the emperor was changed, changed utterly. He rode no more, he hunted no more, he paid no heed to the business of the empire, but remained in seclusion in his own apartments and slept. The court banquets continued without him, music and song he refused to hear, and though in his sleep he smiled and was happy, when he awoke his melancholy could not be cheered or his gloom lightened. When this condition of things had continued for more than a week it was determined that the emperor must be aroused from this dreadful state of apathy, and his groom of the chamber, a noble Roman of very high rank – indeed, a king, under the emperor – resolved to make the endeavour.

'My lord,' said he, 'I have evil tidings for you. The people of Rome are beginning to murmur against you, because of the change that has come over you. They say that you are bewitched, that they can get no answers or decisions from you, and all the affairs of the empire go to wrack and ruin while you sleep and take no heed. You have ceased to be their emperor, they say, and they will cease to be loyal to you.'

The Dream of the Emperor

Then Maxen Wledig roused himself and said to the noble: 'Call hither my wisest senators and councillors, and I will explain the cause of my melancholy, and perhaps they will be able to give me relief.' Accordingly the senators came together, and the emperor ascended his throne, looking so mournful that the whole Senate grieved for him, and feared lest death should speedily overtake him. He began to address them thus:

'Senators and Sages of Rome, I have heard that my people murmur against me, and will rebel if I do not arouse myself. A terrible fate has fallen upon me, and I see no way of escape from my misery, unless ye can find one. It is now more than a week since I went hunting with my court, and when I was wearied I dismounted and slept. In my sleep I dreamt, and a vision cast its spell upon me, so that I feel no happiness unless I am sleeping, and seem to live only in my dreams. I thought I was hunting along the Tiber valley, lost my courtiers, and rode to the head of the valley alone. There the river flowed forth from a great mountain, which looked to me the highest in the world; but I ascended it, and found beyond fair and fertile plains, far vaster than any in our Italy, with mighty rivers flowing through the lovely country to the sea. I followed the course of the greatest river, and reached its mouth, where a noble port stood on the shores of a sea unknown to me. In the harbour lay a fleet of well-appointed ships, and one of these was most beautifully adorned, its planks covered with gold or silver, and its sails of silk. As a gangway of carved ivory led to the deck, I crossed it and entered the vessel, which immediately sailed out of the harbour into the ocean. The voyage was not of long duration, for we soon came to land in a wondrously beautiful island, with scenery of varied loveliness. This island I traversed, led by some secret guidance, till I reached its farthest shore, broken by cliffs and precipices and mountain ranges, while between the mountains and the sea I saw a fair and fruitful land traversed by a silvery, winding river, with a castle at its mouth. My longing drew me to the castle, and when I came to the gate I entered, for the dwelling stood open to every man, and such a hall as was therein I have never seen for splendour, even in Imperial Rome. The walls were covered with gold, set with precious gems, the seats were of gold and the tables of silver, and two fair youths, whom I saw playing chess, used pieces of gold on a board of silver. Their attire was of black satin embroidered with gold, and golden circlets were on their brows. I gazed at the youths for a moment, and next became aware of an aged man sitting near them. His carved ivory seat was adorned with golden eagles, the token of Imperial Rome; his ornaments on arms and hands and neck were of bright gold, and he was carving fresh chessmen from a rod of solid gold. Beside him sat, on a golden chair, a maiden (the loveliest in the whole world she seemed, and still seems, to me). White was her inner dress under a golden overdress, her crown of gold adorned with rubies and pearls, and a golden girdle encircled her slender waist. The beauty of her face won my love in that moment, and I knelt and said: "Hail, Empress of Rome!" but as she bent forward from her seat to greet me I awoke. Now I have no peace and no joy except in sleep, for in dreams I always see my lady, and in dreams we love each other and are happy; therefore in dreams will I live, unless ye can find some way to satisfy my longing while I wake.'

The Quest for the Maiden

The senators were at first greatly amazed, and then one of them said: 'My lord, will you not send out messengers to seek throughout all your lands for the maiden in the castle? Let each group of messengers search for one year, and return at the end of the year with tidings. So shall you live in good hope of success from year to year.' The messengers were sent out accordingly, with wands in their hands and a sleeve tied on each cap, in token of peace and of an embassy; but though they searched with all diligence, after three years three separate embassies had brought back no news of the mysterious land and the beauteous maiden.

Then the groom of the chamber said to Maxen Wledig: 'My lord, will you not go forth to hunt, as on the day when you dreamt this enthralling dream?' To this the emperor agreed, and rode to the place in the valley where he had slept. 'Here,' he said, 'my dream began, and I seemed to follow the river to its source.' Then the groom of the chamber said: 'Will you not send messengers to the river's source, my lord, and bid them follow the track of your dream?' Accordingly thirteen messengers were sent, who followed the river up until it issued from the highest mountain they had ever seen. 'Behold our emperor's dream!' they exclaimed, and they ascended the mountain, and descended the other side into a most beautiful and fertile plain, as Maxen Wledig had seen in his dream. Following the greatest river of all (probably the Rhine), the ambassadors reached the great seaport on the North Sea, and found the fleet waiting with one vessel larger than all the others; and they entered the ship and were carried to the fair island of Britain. Here they journeyed westward, and came to the mountainous land of Snowdon, whence they could see the sacred isle of Mona (Anglesey) and the fertile land of Arvon lying between the mountains and the sea. 'This,' said the messengers, 'is the land of our master's dream, and in yon fair castle we shall find the maiden whom our emperor loves.'

The Finding of the Maiden

So they went through the lovely land of Arvon to the castle of Caernarvon, and in that lordly fortress was the great hall, with the two youths playing chess, the venerable man carving chessmen, and the maiden in her chair of gold. When the ambassadors saw the fair Princess Helena they fell on their knees before her and said: 'Empress of Rome, all hail!' But Helena half rose from her seat in anger as she said. 'What does this mockery mean? You seem to be men of gentle breeding, and you wear the badge of messengers: whence comes it, then, that ye mock me thus?' But the ambassadors calmed her anger, saying: 'Be not wroth, lady: this is no mockery, for the Emperor of Rome, the great lord Maxen Wledig, has seen you in a dream, and he has sworn to wed none but you. Which, therefore, will you choose, to accompany us to Rome, and there be made empress, or to wait here until the emperor can come to you?' The princess thought deeply for a time, and then replied: 'I would not be too credulous, or too hard of belief. If the emperor loves me and would wed me, let him find me in my father's house, and make me his bride in my own home.'

The Dream Realized

After this the thirteen envoys departed, and returned to the emperor in such haste that when their horses failed they gave no heed, but took others and pressed on. When they reached Rome and informed Maxen Wledig of the success of their

mission he at once gathered his army and marched across Europe towards Britain. When the Roman emperor had crossed the sea he conquered Britain from Beli the son of Manogan, and made his way to Arvon. On entering his castle he saw first the two youths, Kynon and Adeon, playing chess, then their father, Eudav, the son of Caradoc, and then his beloved, the beauteous Helena, daughter of Eudav. 'Empress of Rome, all hail!' Maxen Wledig said; and the princess bent forward in her chair and kissed him, for she knew he was her destined husband. The next day they were wedded, and the Emperor Maxen Wledig gave Helena as dowry all Britain for her father, the son of the gallant Caradoc, and for herself three castles, Caernarvon, Caerlleon, and Caermarthen, where she dwelt in turn; and in one of them was born her son Constantine, the only British-born Emperor of Rome. To this day in Wales the old Roman roads that connected Helena's three castles are known as 'Sarn Helen.'

Havelok The Dane

I N THE story of Havelok we have a curious blend of characters and cultures. Havelok probably began life as a Welsh hero named Ablac who subsequently became confused with Olaf Sigtryggson (also called Cuaran), the Danish king of Dublin from 945–80. He also had a claim to the kingdom of Northumbria but was three times driven out from there, possibly giving rise to the confusion with the disinherited hero Havelok. Olaf is later said to have married the daughter of King Constantine III of Scotland and was thus related to King Athelstan of England. However, this may well refer to his brother Olaf Gothfrithson. On to the life of this historical character has been grafted the ancient theme of the disinherited hero who regains his rightful place after many adventures.

As M. I. Ebbutt himself pointed out in his original introduction to the story, 'Kings who die leaving helpless heirs to the guardianship of ambitious and wicked nobles were not rare in the early days of Britain, Wales, or Denmark; the murder of the heir and the usurpation of the kingdom by the cruel regent were no unusual occurrences.' This may have influenced the continuing currency of the story, especially once it became linked with the local folk history of the Midlands.

The text from which the story derives also contains 'King Horn' and the two are often printed together and considered in the same breath. This is in some ways unfortunate as *The Lay of Havelok* is in many ways a more interesting story, and as such deserves to be better known. The following extract (in slightly modernized English) serves to give the flavour of the original, showing both the piety (*sic*) of its author, and the fact that he is evidently telling the tale to an audience of peasants.

Hearken to me good men,
Wives, maidens, and all men,
Of a tale that I shall you tell
Who-so it wills here to dwell.
The tale is of Havelok I make
That while he was little, was ill-clothed.
Havelok was a full good man,
He was full good in any troop;
He was the strongest man at need
That might ever ride on any steed.
So that you learn what now you hear,
At the beginning of our tale,
Fill me a cup of full good ale;
And while I drink, here will relate
That Christ shields us all from Hell!
Christ left us ever so for to do,
That we might come unto him to;
And with hope that it might be so
Benedicamus Domino!

In all there are four versions of the story. The first is contained in the historical chronicle *Estoire des Engles* by Geoffrey Gaimer (*c.* 1150); the second in the Old French *Lai d'Havelok*; the third is the poem retold here, and the fourth a brief summary of the present poem contained in the translation of Peter Langtoft's fifteenth-century *Chronicle*, translated by Robert Manning of Brunne (Bourne, in Lincolnshire). This attests to the considerable popularity of the story, extending from the twelfth to the fourteenth centuries.

Unlike 'The Dream of Maxen Wledig' where the relationship of king to land is blessed by the earthly representative of the goddess, Havelok's kingship is ratified by God, who watches over the monarch and several times intervenes in his life, causing the mysterious light which issues from his mouth, and later on the sign of the cross which appears on his shoulder. In this way Havelok is distinguished as a king whose qualities are sanctified by the heavenly monarch and who reflects his deity in human terms.

This is not really surprising since the work was written down by a Christian monk who may well have sought (as so often occurs) to improve the original story and Christianize its hero, as well as taking the opportunity to elaborate on the theme of human kingship: the earthly king compared to the heavenly king. Havelok's character, which exhibits humility and grace, certainly lends itself to this treatment, though he may not always have been pictured in this way.

Another unusual aspect of the story is that, despite being couched in the language of 'courtly' romances, it is by no means typical of this genre. Rather it is a 'peasant' romance which concerns itself very much with the lot of the poor, especially as represented in the character of the fisherman Grimm – here supposed to have given his name to the town of Grimsby. Nevertheless, while the poem may not be a courtly epic in the true sense of the word, it is undoubtedly a chivalric one, with all of Havelok's prowess and honourable nature being fully acknowledged. In this way he becomes, in fact, a far more believable figure than some of the heroes of Arthurian or courtly fiction, where the *raison d'être* of every knight is to undertake a quest and be challenged to the utmost by the adventures he meets along the way. Havelok, on the other hand, undertakes adventures which are presented to him by circumstances in his life. He does not actively seek out adventure in the manner of, say, Gawain or Lancelot in the more conventional Arthurian literature of the time.

Havelok is actually set in the tenth century but, as was customary when the story was recorded, it is dressed in the costume and manners of the time – in this instance the thirteenth-century world of heroic chivalry.

Havelok and Godard

In Denmark, long ago, lived a good king named Birkabeyn, rich and powerful, a great warrior and a man of mighty prowess, whose rule was undisputed over the whole realm. He had three children – two daughters, named Swanborow and Elfleda the Fair, and one young and goodly son, Havelok, the heir to all his dominions. All too soon came the day that no man can avoid, when Death would call King Birkabeyn away, and he grieved sore over his young children to be left fatherless and unprotected; but, after much reflection, and prayers to God for wisdom to help his choice, he called to him Jarl Godard, a trusted counsellor and friend, and committed into his hands the care of the realm and of the three royal children, until Havelok should be of age to be knighted and rule the land himself. King Birkabeyn felt that such a charge was too great a temptation for any man unbound by oaths of fealty and honour, and although he did not distrust his friend, he required Godard to swear,

> By altar and by holy service book,
> By bells that call the faithful to the church,
> By blessed sacrament, and sacred rites,
> By Holy Rood, and Him who died thereon,
> That thou wilt truly rule and keep my realm,
> Wilt guard my babes in love and loyalty,
> Until my son be grown, and dubbed knight:
> That thou wilt then resign to him his land,
> His power and rule, and all that owns his sway.

Jarl Godard took this most solemn oath at once, with many protestations of affection and whole-hearted devotion to the dying king and his heir, and King Birkabeyn died happy in the thought that his children would be well cared for during their helpless youth.

When the funeral rites were celebrated Jarl Godard assumed the rule of the country, and, under pretext of securing the safety of the royal children, removed them to a strong castle, where no man was allowed access to them, and where they were kept so closely that the royal residence became a prison in all but name. Godard, finding Denmark submit to his government without resistance, began to adopt measures to rid himself of the real heirs to the throne, and gave orders that food and clothes should be supplied to the three children in such scanty quantities that they might die of hardship; but since they were slow to succumb to this cruel, torturing form of murder, he resolved to slay them suddenly, knowing that no one durst call him to account. Having steeled his heart against all pitiful thoughts, he went to the castle, and was taken to the inner dungeon where the poor babes lay shivering and weeping for cold and hunger. As he entered, Havelok, who was even then a bold lad, greeted him courteously, and knelt before him, with clasped hands, begging a boon.

'Why do you weep and wail so sore?' asked Godard.

'Because we are so hungry,' answered Havelok. 'We have so little food, and we have no servants to wait on us; they do not give us half as much as we could eat; we are shivering with cold, and our clothes are all in rags. Woe to us that we were ever born! Is there in the land no more corn with which men can make bread for us? We are nearly dead from hunger.'

These pathetic words had no effect on Godard, who had resolved to yield to no pity and show no mercy. He seized the two little girls as they lay cowering together, clasping one another for warmth, and cut their throats, letting the bodies of the hapless babies fall to the floor in a pool of blood; and then, turning to Havelok, aimed his knife at the boy's heart. The poor child, terrified by the awful fate of the two girls, knelt again before him and begged for mercy:

> 'Fair lord, have mercy on me now, I pray!
> Look on my helpless youth, and pity me!
> Oh, let me live, and I will yield you all –
> My realm of Denmark will I leave to you,
> And swear that I will ne'er assail your sway.
> Oh, pity me, lord! be compassionate!
> And I will flee far from this land of mine,
> And vow that Birkabeyn was ne'er my sire!'

Jarl Godard was touched by Havelok's piteous speech, and felt some faint compassion, so that he could not slay the lad himself; yet he knew that his only safety was in Havelok's death.

'If I let him go,' thought he, 'Havelok will at last work me woe! I shall have no peace in my life, and my children after me will not hold the lordship of Denmark in safety, if Havelok escapes! Yet I cannot slay him with my own hands. I will have him cast into the sea with an anchor about his neck: thus at least his body will not float.'

Godard left Havelok kneeling in terror, and, striding from the tower, leaving the door locked behind him, he sent for an ignorant fisherman, Grim, who, he thought, could be frightened into doing his will. When Grim came he was led into an ante-room, where Godard, with terrible look and voice, addressed him thus:

'Grim, thou knowest thou art my thrall.' 'Yea, fair lord,' quoth Grim, trembling at Godard's stern voice. 'And I can slay thee if thou dost disobey me.' 'Yea, lord; but how have I offended you?' 'Thou hast not yet; but I have a task for thee, and if thou dost it not, dire punishment shall fall upon thee.' 'Lord, what is the work that I must do?' asked the poor fisherman. 'Tarry: I will show thee.' Then Godard went into the inner room of the tower, whence he returned leading a fair boy, who wept bitterly. 'Take this boy secretly to thy house, and keep him there till dead of night; then launch thy boat, row out to sea, and fling him therein with an anchor round his neck, so that I shall see him never again.'

Grim looked curiously at the weeping boy, and said: 'What reward shall I have if I work this sin for you?'

Godard replied: 'The sin will be on my head, as I am thy lord and bid thee do it; but I will make thee a freeman, noble and rich, and my friend, if thou wilt do this secretly and discreetly.'

Thus reassured and bribed, Grim suddenly took the boy, flung him to the ground, and bound him hand and foot with cord which he took from his pockets. So anxious was he to secure the boy that he drew the cords very tight, and Havelok suffered terrible pain; he could not cry out, for a handful of rags was thrust into his mouth and over his nostrils, so that he could hardly breathe. Then Grim flung the poor boy into a horrible black sack, and carried him thus from the castle, as if he were bringing home broken food for his family. When Grim reached his poor cottage, where his wife Leve was waiting for him, he slung the sack from his shoulder and gave it to her, saying, 'Take good care of this boy as of thy life.

I am to drown him at midnight, and if I do so my lord has promised to make me a freeman and give me great wealth.'

When Dame Leve heard this she sprang up and flung the lad down in a corner, and nearly broke his head with the crash against the earthen floor. There Havelok lay, bruised and aching, while the couple went to sleep, leaving the room all dark but for the red glow from the fire. At midnight Grim awoke to do his lord's behest, and Dame Leve, going to the living-room to kindle a light, was terrified by a mysterious gleam as bright as day which shone around the boy on the floor and streamed from his mouth. Leve hastily called Grim to see this wonder, and together they released Havelok from the gag and bonds and examined his body, when they found on the right shoulder the token of true royalty, a cross of red gold.

'God knows,' quoth Grim, 'that this is the heir of our land. He will come to rule in good time, will bear sway over England and Denmark, and will punish the cruel Godard.' Then, weeping sore, the loyal fisherman fell down at Havelok's feet, crying, 'Lord, have mercy on me and my wife! We are thy thralls, and never will we do aught against thee. We will nourish thee until thou canst rule, and will hide thee from Godard; and thou wilt perchance give me my freedom in return for thy life.'

At this unexpected address Havelok sat up surprised, and rubbed his bruised head and said: 'I am nearly dead, what with hunger, and thy cruel bonds, and the gag. Now bring me food in plenty!' 'Yea, lord,' said Dame Leve, and bustled about, bringing the best they had in the hut; and Havelok ate as if he had fasted for three days; and then he was put to bed, and slept in peace while Grim watched over him.

However, Grim went the next morning to Jarl Godard and said: 'Lord, I have done your behest, and drowned the boy with an anchor about his neck. He is safe, and now, I pray you, give me my reward, the gold and other treasures, and make me a freeman as you have promised.' But Godard only looked fiercely at him and said: 'What, wouldst thou be an earl? Go home, thou foul churl, and be ever a thrall! It is enough reward that I do not hang thee now for insolence, and for thy wicked deeds. Go speedily, else thou mayst stand and palter with me too long.' And Grim shrank quietly away, lest Godard should slay him for the murder of Havelok.

Now Grim saw in what a terrible plight he stood, at the mercy of this cruel and treacherous man, and he took counsel with himself and consulted his wife, and the two decided to flee from Denmark to save their lives. Gradually Grim sold all his stock, his cattle, his nets, everything that he owned, and turned it into good pieces of gold; then he bought and secretly fitted out and provisioned a ship, and at last, when all was ready, carried on board Havelok (who had lain hidden all this time), his own three sons and two daughters; then when he and his wife had gone on board he set sail, and, driven by a favourable wind, reached the shores of England.

Goldborough and Earl Godrich

Meanwhile in England a somewhat similar fate had befallen a fair princess named Goldborough. When her father, King Athelwold, lay dying all his people mourned, for he was the flower of all fair England for knighthood, justice, and mercy; and he himself grieved sorely for the sake of his little daughter, soon to be left an orphan. 'What will she do?' moaned he. 'She can neither speak nor walk! If she were only

'Havelok sat up surprised'

able to ride, to rule England, and to guard herself from shame, I should have no grief, even if I died and left her alone, while I lived in the joy of paradise!'

Then Athelwold summoned a council to be held at Winchester, and asked the advice of the nobles as to the care of the infant Goldborough. They with one accord recommended Earl Godrich of Cornwall to be made regent for the little princess; and the earl, on being appointed, swore with all solemn rites that he would marry her at twelve years old to the highest, the best, fairest, and strongest man alive, and in the meantime would train her in all royal virtues and customs. So King Athelwold died, and was buried with great lamentations, and Godrich ruled the land as regent. He was a strict but just governor, and England had great peace, without and within, under his severe rule, for all lived in awe of him, though no man loved him. Goldborough grew and throve in all ways, and became famous through the land for her gracious beauty and gentle and virtuous demeanour. This roused the jealousy of Earl Godrich, who had played the part of king so long that he almost believed himself King of England, and he began to consider how he could secure the kingdom for himself and his son. Thereupon he had Goldborough taken from Winchester, where she kept royal state, to Dover, where she was imprisoned in the castle, and strictly secluded from all her friends; there she remained, with poor clothes and scanty food, awaiting a champion to uphold her right.

Havelok Becomes Cook's Boy

When Grim sailed from Denmark to England he landed in the Humber, at the place now called Grimsby, and there established himself as a fisherman. So successful was he that for twelve years he supported his family well, and carried his catches of fish far afield, even to Lincoln, where rare fish always brought a good price. In all this time Grim never once called on Havelok for help in the task of feeding the family; he reverenced his king, and the whole household served Havelok with the utmost deference, and often went with scanty rations to satisfy the boy's great appetite. At length Havelok began to think how selfishly he was living, and how much food he consumed, and was filled with shame when he realized how his foster-father toiled unweariedly while he did nothing to help. In his remorseful meditations it became clear to him that, though a king's son, he ought to do some useful work. 'Of what use,' thought he, 'is my great strength and stature if I do not employ it for some good purpose? There is no shame in honest toil. I will work for my food, and try to make some return to Father Grim, who has done so much for me. I will gladly bear his baskets of fish to market, and I will begin to-morrow.'

On the next day, in spite of Grim's protests, Havelok carried a load of fish equal to four men's burden to Grimsby market, and sold it successfully, returning home with the money he received; and this he did day by day, till a famine arose and fish and food both became scarce. Then Grim, more concerned for Havelok than for his own children, called the youth to him and bade him try his fortunes in Lincoln, for his own sake and for theirs; he would be better fed, and the little food Grim could get would go further among the others if Havelok were not there. The one obstacle in the way was Havelok's lack of clothes, and Grim overcame that by sacrificing his boat's sail to make Havelok a coarse tunic. That done, they bade each other farewell, and Havelok started for Lincoln, barefooted and bareheaded, for his only garment was the sailcloth tunic. In Lincoln Havelok found no friends and no food for two days, and he was desperate and faint with hunger, when he heard a call: 'Porters, porters! hither to me!' Roused to new vigour by the chance of work, Havelok rushed with the rest, and bore down and hurled aside the other porters so vigorously that he was chosen to carry provisions for Bertram, the earl's cook; and in return he received the first meal he had eaten for nearly three days.

On the next day Havelok again overthrew the porters, and, knocking down at least sixteen, secured the work. This time he had to carry fish, and his basket was so laden that he bore nearly a cartload, with which he ran to the castle. There the cook, amazed at his strength, first gave him a hearty meal, and then offered him good service under himself, with food and lodging for his wages. This offer Havelok accepted, and was installed as cook's boy, and employed in all the lowest offices – carrying wood, water, turf, hewing logs, lifting, fetching, carrying – and in all he showed himself a wonderfully strong worker, with unfailing good temper and gentleness, so that the little children all loved the big, gentle, fair-haired youth who worked so quietly and played with them so merrily. When Havelok's old tunic became worn out, his master, the cook, took pity on him and gave him a new suit, and then it could be seen how handsome and tall and strong a youth this cook's boy really was, and his fame spread far and wide round Lincoln Town.

Havelok and Goldborough

At the great fair of Lincoln, sports of all kinds were indulged in, and in these Havelok took his part, for the cook, proud of his mighty scullion, urged him to compete in all the games and races. As Earl Godrich had summoned his Parliament to meet that year at Lincoln, there was a great concourse of spectators, and even the powerful Earl Regent himself sometimes watched the sports and cheered the champions. The first contest was 'putting the stone,' and the stone chosen was so weighty that none but the most stalwart could lift it above the knee – none could raise it to his breast. This sport was new to Havelok, who had never seen it before, but when the cook bade him try his strength he lifted the stone easily and threw it more than twelve feet. This mighty deed caused his fame to be spread, not only among the poor servants with whom Havelok was classed, but also among the barons, their masters, and Havelok's Stone became a landmark in Lincoln. Thus Godrich heard of a youth who stood head and shoulders taller than other men, and was stronger, more handsome – and yet a mere common scullion. The news brought him a flash of inspiration: 'Here is the highest, strongest, best man in all England, and him shall Goldborough wed. I shall keep my vow to the letter, and England must fall to me, for Goldborough's royal blood will be lost by her marriage with a thrall, the people will refuse her obedience, and England will cast her out.'

Godrich therefore brought Goldborough to Lincoln, received her with bell-ringing and seemly rejoicing, and bade her prepare for her wedding. This the princess refused to do until she knew who was her destined husband, for she said she would wed no man who was not of royal birth. Her firmness drove Earl Godrich to fierce wrath, and he burst out: 'Wilt thou be queen and mistress over me? Thy pride shall be brought down: thou shalt have no royal spouse: a vagabond and scullion shalt thou wed, and that no later than to-morrow! Curses on him who speaks thee fair!' In vain the princess wept and bemoaned herself: the wedding was fixed for the morrow morn.

The next day at dawn Earl Godrich sent for Havelok, the mighty cook's boy, and asked him: 'Wilt thou take a wife?'

'Nay,' quoth Havelok, 'that will I not. I cannot feed her, much less clothe and lodge her. My very garments are not my own, but belong to the cook, my master.' Godrich fell upon Havelok and beat him furiously, saying, 'Unless thou wilt take the wench I give thee for wife I will hang or blind thee'; and so, in great fear, Havelok agreed to the wedding. At once Goldborough was brought, and forced into an immediate marriage, under penalty of banishment or burning as a witch if she refused. And thus the unwilling couple were united by the Archbishop of York, who had come to attend the Parliament.

Never was there so sad a wedding! The people murmured greatly at this unequal union; and pitied the poor princess, thus driven to wed a man of low birth; and Goldborough herself wept pitifully, but resigned herself to God's will. All men now acknowledged with grief that she and her husband could have no claim to the English throne, and thus Godrich seemed to have gained his object. Havelok and his unwilling bride recognized that they would not be safe near Godrich, and as Havelok had no home in Lincoln to which he could take the princess, he determined to go back to his faithful foster-father, Grim, and put the fair young bride under his loyal protection. Sorrowfully, with grief and shame in their hearts, Havelok and Goldborough made their way on foot to Grimsby, only to find the loyal Grim dead; but his five children were alive and in prosperity. When they saw Havelok and his wife they fell on their knees and saluted them with all respect and reverence. In their joy to see their king again, these worthy fisherfolk forgot their newly won wealth, and said: 'Welcome, dear lord, and thy fair lady! What joy is ours to see thee again, for thy subjects are we, and thou canst do with us as thou wilt. All that we have is thine, and if thou wilt dwell with us we will serve thee and thy wife truly in all ways!' This greeting surprised Goldborough, who began to suspect some mystery, and she was greatly comforted when brothers and sisters busied themselves in lighting fires, cooking meals, and waiting on her hand and foot, as if she had been indeed a king's wife. Havelok, however, said nothing to explain the mystery, and Goldborough that night lay awake bewailing her fate as a thrall's bride, even though he was the fairest man in England.

The Revelation and Return to Denmark

As Goldborough lay sleepless and unhappy she became aware of a brilliant light shining around Havelok, and streaming from his mouth; and while she feared and wondered an angelic voice cried to her:

> 'Fair Princess, cease this grief and heavy moan!
> For Havelok, thy newly wedded spouse,
> Is son and heir to famous kings: the sign
> Thou findest in the cross of ruddy gold
> That shineth on his shoulder. He shall be
> Monarch and ruler of two mighty realms;
> Denmark and England shall obey his rule,
> And he shall sway them with a sure command.
> This shalt thou see with thine own eyes, and be
> Lady and Queen, with Havelok, o'er these lands.'

This angelic message so gladdened Goldborough that she kissed, for the first time, her unconscious husband, who started up from his sleep, saying, 'Dear love, sleepest thou? I have had a wondrous dream. I thought I sat on a lofty hill, and saw all Denmark before me. As I stretched out my arms I embraced it all, and the people clung to my arms, and the castles fell at my feet; then I flew over the salt sea with the Danish people clinging to me, and I closed all fair England in my hand, and gave it to thee, dear love! Now what can this mean?'

Goldborough answered joyfully: 'It means, dear heart, that thou shalt be King of Denmark and of England too: all these realms shall fall into thy power, and thou shalt be ruler in Denmark within one year. Now do thou follow my advice, and let us go to Denmark taking with us Grim's three sons, who will accompany thee for love and loyalty; and have no fear, for I know thou wilt succeed.'

The next morning Havelok went to church early, and prayed humbly and heartily for success in his enterprise and retribution on the false traitor Godard; then, laying his offering on the altar before the Cross, he went away glad in heart. Grim's three sons, Robert the Red, William Wendut, and Hugh the Raven, joyfully consented to go with Havelok to Denmark, to attack with all their power the false Jarl Godard and to win the kingdom for the rightful heir. Their wives and families stayed in England, but Goldborough would not leave her husband, and after a short voyage the party landed safely on the shores of Denmark, in the lands of Jarl Ubbe, an old friend of King Birkabeyn, who lived far from the court now that a usurper held sway in Denmark.

Havelok and Ubbe

Havelok dared not reveal himself and his errand until he knew more of the state of parties in the country, and he therefore only begged permission to live and trade there, giving Ubbe, as a token of goodwill and a tribute to his power, a valuable ring, which the jarl prized greatly. Ubbe, gazing at the so-called merchant's great stature and beauty, lamented that he was not of noble birth, and planned to persuade him to take up the profession of arms. At first, however, he simply granted Havelok permission to trade, and invited him and Goldborough to a feast, promising them safety and honour under his protection. Havelok dreaded lest his wife's beauty might place them in jeopardy, but he dared not refuse the invitation, which was pointedly given to both; accordingly, when they went to Ubbe's hall, Goldborough was escorted by Robert the Red and William Wendut.

Ubbe received them with all honour, and all men marvelled at Goldborough's beauty, and Ubbe's wife loved Goldborough at first sight as her husband did Havelok, so that the feast passed off with all joy and mirth, and none dared raise a hand or lift his voice against the wandering merchant whom Ubbe so strangely favoured. But Ubbe knew that when once Havelok and his wife were away from his protection there would be little safety for them, since the rough Danish nobles would think nothing of stealing a trader's fair wife, and many a man had cast longing eyes on Goldborough's loveliness. Therefore when the feast was over, and Havelok took his leave, Ubbe sent with him a body of ten knights and sixty men-at-arms, and recommended them to the magistrate of the town, Bernard Brown, a true and upright man, bidding him, as he prized his life, keep the strangers in safety and honour. Well it was that Ubbe and Bernard Brown took these precautions, for

late at night a riotous crowd came to Bernard's house clamouring for admittance. Bernard withstood the angry mob, armed with a great axe, but they burst the door in by hurling a huge stone; and then Havelok joined in the defence. He drew out the great beam which barred the door, and crying, 'Come quickly to me, and you shall stay here! Curses on him who flees!' began to lay about him with the big beam, so that three fell dead at once. A terrible fight followed, in which Havelok, armed only with the beam, slew twenty men in armour, and was then sore beset by the rest of the troop, aiming darts and arrows at his unarmoured breast. It was going hardly with him, when Hugh the Raven, hearing and understanding the cries of the assailants, called his brothers to their lord's aid, and they all joined the fight so furiously that, long ere day, of the sixty men who had attacked the inn not one remained alive.

In the morning news was brought to Jarl Ubbe that his stranger guest had slain sixty of the best of his soldiery.

'What can this mean?' said Ubbe. 'I had better go and see to it myself, for any messenger would surely treat Havelok discourteously, and I should be full loath to do that.' He rode away to the house of Bernard Brown, and asked the meaning of its damaged and battered appearance.

'My lord,' answered Bernard Brown, 'last night at moonrise there came a band of sixty thieves who would have plundered my house and bound me hand and foot. When Havelok and his companions saw it they came to my aid, with sticks and stones, and drove out the robbers like dogs from a mill. Havelok himself slew three at one blow. Never have I seen a warrior so good! He is worth a thousand in a fray. But alas! he is grievously wounded, with three deadly gashes in side and arm and thigh, and at least twenty smaller wounds. I am scarcely harmed at all, but I fear he will die full soon.'

Ubbe could scarcely believe so strange a tale, but all the bystanders swore that Bernard told nothing but the bare truth, and that the whole gang of thieves, with their leader, Griffin the Welshman, had been slain by the hero and his small party. Then Ubbe bade them bring Havelok, that he might call a leech to heal his wounds, for if the stranger merchant should live Jarl Ubbe would without fail dub him knight; and when the leech had seen the wounds he said the patient would make a good and quick recovery. Then Ubbe offered Havelok and his wife a dwelling in his own castle, under his own protection, till Havelok's grievous wounds were healed. There, too, fair Goldborough would be under the care of Ubbe's wife, who would cherish her as her own daughter. This kind offer was accepted gladly, and they all went to the castle, where a room was given them next to Ubbe's own.

At midnight Ubbe woke, aroused by a bright light in Havelok's room, which was only separated from his own by a slight wooden partition. He was vexed, suspecting his guest of midnight wassailing, and went to inquire what villainy might be hatching. To his surprise, both husband and wife were sound asleep, but the light shone from Havelok's mouth, and made a glory round his head. Utterly amazed at the marvel, Ubbe went away silently, and returned with all the garrison of his castle to the room where his guests still lay sleeping. As they gazed on the light Havelok turned in his sleep, and they saw on his shoulder the golden cross, shining like the sun, which all men knew to be the token of royal birth. Then Ubbe exclaimed: 'Now I know who this is, and why I loved him so dearly at first sight: this is the son of our dead King Birkabeyn. Never was man so like another as this man is to the dead king: he is his very image and his true heir.' With great joy they fell on their knees and kissed him eagerly, and Havelok awoke and began to scowl furiously, for he thought it was some treacherous attack; but Ubbe soon undeceived him.

> '"Dear lord," quoth he, "be thou in naught dismayed,
> For in thine eyes methinks I see thy thought –
> Dear son, great joy is mine to live this day!
> My homage, lord, I freely offer thee:
> Thy loyal men and vassals are we all,
> For thou art son of mighty Birkabeyn,
> And soon shalt conquer all thy father's land,
> Though thou art young and almost friendless here.
> To-morrow will we swear our fealty due,
> And dub thee knight, for prowess unexcelled."'

Now Havelok knew that his worst danger was over, and he thanked God for the friend He had sent him, and left to the good Jarl Ubbe the management of his cause. Ubbe gathered an assembly of as many mighty men of the realm, and barons, and good citizens, as he could summon; and when they were all assembled, wondering what was the cause of this imperative summons, Ubbe arose and said:

'Gentles, bear with me if I tell you first things well known to you. Ye know that King Birkabeyn ruled this land until his death-day, and that he left three children – one son, Havelok, and two daughters – to the guardianship of Jarl Godard: ye all heard him swear to keep them loyally and treat them well. But ye do not know how he kept his oath! The false traitor slew both the maidens, and would have slain the boy, but for pity he would not kill the child with his own hands. He bade a fisherman drown him in the sea; but when the good man knew that it was the rightful heir, he saved the boy's life and fled with him to England, where Havelok has been brought up for many years. And now, behold! here he stands. In all the world he has no peer, and ye may well rejoice in the beauty and manliness of your king. Come now and pay homage to Havelok, and I myself will be your leader!'

Jarl Ubbe turned to Havelok, where he stood with Goldborough beside him, and knelt before him to do homage, an example which was followed by all present. At a second and still larger assembly held a fortnight later a similar oath of fealty was sworn by all, Havelok was dubbed knight by the noble Ubbe, and a great festival was celebrated, with sports and amusements for the populace. A council of war and vengeance was held with the great nobles.

The Death of Godard

Havelok, now acknowledged King of Denmark, was unsatisfied until he had punished the treacherous Godard, and he took a solemn oath from his soldiers that they would never cease the search for the traitor till they had captured him and brought him bound to judgment. After all, Godard was captured as he was hunting. Grim's three sons, now knighted by King Havelok, met him in the forest, and bade him come to the king, who called on him to remember and account for his treatment of Birkabeyn's children. Godard struck out furiously with his fists, but Sir Robert the Red wounded him in the right arm. When Godard's men joined in the combat, Robert and his brothers soon slew ten of their adversaries, and the rest fled; returning, ashamed at the bitter reproaches of their lord, they were all slain by Havelok's men. Godard was taken, bound hand and foot, placed on a miserable jade with his face to the tail, and so led to Havelok. The king refused to be the judge of his own cause, and entrusted to Ubbe the task of presiding at the traitor's trial. No mercy was shown to the cruel Jarl Godard, and he was condemned to a traitor's death, with torments of terrible barbarity. The sentence was carried out to the letter, and Denmark rejoiced in the punishment of a cruel villain.

Death of Godrich

Meanwhile Earl Godrich of Cornwall had heard with great uneasiness that Havelok had become King of Denmark, and intended to invade England with a mighty army to assert his wife's right to the throne. He recognized that his own device to shame Goldborough had turned against him, and that he must now fight for his life and the usurped dominion he held over England. Godrich summoned his army to Lincoln for the defence of the realm against the Danes, and called out every man fit to bear weapons, on pain of becoming thrall if they failed him. Then he thus addressed them:

> 'Friends, listen to my words, and you will know
> 'Tis not for sport, nor idle show, that I
> Have bidden you to meet at Lincoln here.
> Lo! here at Grimsby foreigners are come
> Who have already won the Priory.
> These Danes are cruel heathen, who destroy
> Our churches and our abbeys: priests and nuns
> They torture to the death, or lead away
> To serve as slaves the haughty Danish jarls.
> Now, Englishmen, what counsel will ye take?
> If we submit, they will rule all our land,
> Will kill us all, and sell our babes for thralls,
> Will take our wives and daughters for their own.
> Help me, if ever ye loved English land,
> To fight these heathen and to cleanse our soil
> From hateful presence of these alien hordes.
> I make my vow to God and all the saints
> I will not rest, nor houseled be, nor shriven,
> Until our realm be free from Danish foe!
> Accursed be he who strikes no blow for home!'

The army was inspired with valour by these courageous words, and the march to Grimsby began at once, with Earl Godrich in command. Havelok's men marched out gallantly to meet them, and when the battle joined many mighty deeds of valour were done, especially by the king himself, his foster-brothers, and Jarl Ubbe. The battle lasted long and was very fierce and bloody but the Danes gradually overcame the resistance of the English, and at last, after a great hand-to-hand conflict, King Havelok captured Godrich. The traitor earl, who had lost a hand in the fray, was sent bound and fettered to Queen Goldborough, who kept him, carefully guarded, until he could be tried by his peers, since (for all his treason) he was still a knight.

When the English recognized their rightful lady and queen they did homage with great joy, begging mercy for having resisted their lawful ruler at the command of a wicked traitor; and the king and queen pardoned all but Godrich, who was speedily brought to trial at Lincoln. He was sentenced to be burnt at the stake, and the sentence was carried out amid general rejoicings.

Now that vengeance was satisfied, Havelok and his wife thought of recompensing the loyal helpers who had believed in them and supported them through the long years of adversity. Havelok married one of Grim's daughters to the Earl of Chester, and the other to Bertram, the good cook, who became Earl of Cornwall in the place of the felon Godrich and his disinherited children; the heroic Ubbe was made Regent of Denmark for Havelok, who decided to stay and rule England, and all the noble Danish warriors were rewarded with gifts of gold, and lands and castles. After a great coronation feast, which lasted for forty days, King Havelok dismissed the Danish regent and his followers, and after sad farewells they returned to their own country. Havelok and Goldborough ruled England in peace and security for sixty years, and lived together in all bliss, and had fifteen children, who all became mighty kings and queens.

Cuchulain
the Champion of Ireland

CUCHULAIN is probably Ireland's most famous hero (with Fionn McCumhail a close second). Born to Dechtire, the daughter of one of the Druids, Cathbad, and the god Lugh Lamhfada after the former was carried off to the Otherworld by a flock of bird maidens, he was named Setanta. He gained his nickname, which means 'Hound of Culan' or as it is sometimes written 'Hound of Ulster', after killing the hound of the smith Culan with his bare hands at the age of eight, Culan was so angered by this that Setanta promised to guard his house until he trained another dog, so that he became, in effect, Culan's 'hound'.

Famed for his battle frenzy, in which he underwent a terrifying physical change, Cuchulain soon established his reputation as a hero, achieving a number of astonishing feats of strength and daring. As a youth his battle madness was such that on one occasion, as he returned from a foray with the heads of his enemies decorating his chariot, the only way that he could be calmed down was to be dipped in three tubs of icy water. The first of these burst, the second boiled over, but the third was only warmed by his immersion.

Cuchulain is variously described as having hair of three different colours, four colourful dimples on his cheeks, seven pupils in each eye, and seven fingers and toes on each hand and foot. He possessed various magical weapons, including the 'Gae-Bolg', a fearsome spear which would tear through its victim and return magically to Cuchulain's hand. The two horses which pulled his chariot, the Grey of Macha and the Black of Sainglend, were both possessed of supernatural speed and stamina.

His famous love-match with Emer, daughter of Forgall the Wily, began with a spirited series of riddles, each of which Cuchulain was able to answer.

Emer then sent him forth to be properly trained as a warrior. Quickly outgrowing the teacher to whom he was sent, the youthful hero went on to be trained by the famous woman warrior Scathach, with whose daughter he had a brief affair before he returned to Emer and successfully conquered her.

Women, indeed, found Cuchulain irresistible and always willing to oblige them in matters of love. One text describes him as 'too handsome, too brave, and too young'. His life, however, was dogged with bad luck after he refused the advances of the fearsome battle goddess, the Morrigan, who afterwards plotted his death. After many adventures he finally met his death defending Ulster single-handedly against the forces of Connacht. When he was too weak from loss of blood to stand any longer, he tied himself to a pillar and fought on. When he was finally dead, no one dared approach him until the Morrigan herself, in the form of a crow, settled on his shoulder and an otter began to lap his blood. During the battle Cuchulain was forced to slay his best friend Ferdia who was the champion of the opposing side.

The great cycle of tales which constelled around the figure of Cuchulain and the 'Red Branch Heroes' forms one of the most substantial myth cycles of the Celts. They are filled with magic, warfare, love and tragedy, which have continued to make them among the most popular myths for retelling. Many of the themes found within this cycle echo those of Classical Greece – from which Cuchulain has sometimes come to be termed 'the Irish Achilles' due to the many similarities to be found between the two heroes. The stories were preserved by monkish scribes at Clonmacnoise and Kildare – a fact which makes the magical and pagan element they contain all the more surprising. However, in at least one of these tales Cuchulain appeared in ghostly form to encourage one of his descendants to follow the way of Christ.

The original stories date from the seventh century or even earlier, and almost certainly contain material of a more primitive kind. The most famous story of all is 'The Tain', sometimes also known as 'The Cattle Raid of Cooley', which concerns itself with one of the favourite activities of the early Irish warrior class: cattle-thieving. The resulting war between Ulster and Connacht ended with the death of Cuchulain himself.

The story retold here is based primarily on two texts. The first, which relates the birth of the hero, is the medieval *Book of the Dun Cow*. The second, probably the most famous of the sagas dealing with Cuchulain, is '*Fled Bricriu*' or 'Bricru's Feast' in which the story of the 'Beheading Game' was later immortalized in the fourteenth-century English poem 'Sir Gawain and the Green Knight'.

There have been many translations of the original stories. One of the best is still that of Lady Augusta Gregory, from which the following extract is taken. Here the mischievous Bricriu describes the Champion's Portion to Laegaire:

'Well,' said Bricriu, 'if you can get the Champion's Portion at the feast in my house, the championship of Ireland will be yours for ever. And the Champion's Portion of my house is worth fighting for,' he said, 'for it is not the portion of a fool's house. There goes with it a vat of good wine, with room enough to hold three of the brave men of Ulster; with that a seven year old boar, that has been fed since it was born on no other thing but fresh milk, and fine meal in spring-time, curds and sweet milk in summer, the kernel of nuts and wheat in harvest, beef and broth in the winter; with a seven year old bullock that never had in its mouth, since it was a suckling calf, either heather or twig tops, but only sweet milk and herbs, meadow hay and corn; along with that, five score wheaten cakes made with honey. And since you are yourself the best hero among the men of Ulster,' he said, 'it is but right to give it to you; and that is my wish, you to get it.'

The Youth of Cuchulain

Cuchulain was the nephew of King Conor of Ulster, son of his sister Dechtire, and men say his father was no mortal man, but the great god Lugh of the Long Hand. When Cuchulain was born he was brought up by King Conor himself and the wisest men of Ireland; when five years old, he beat all the other boys in games and warlike exercises, and on the day on which he was seven he assumed the arms of a warrior, so much greater was he than the sons of mortal men. Cuchulain had overheard his tutor, Cathbad the Druid, say to the older youths, 'If any young man take arms to-day, his name will be greater than any other name in Ireland, but his span of life will be short,' and as he loved fame above long life, he persuaded his uncle, King Conor, to invest him with the weapon of manhood. His fame soon spread all over Ireland, for his warlike deeds were those of a proved warrior, not of a child of nursery age, and by the time Cuchulain was seventeen he was in reality without peer among the champions of Ulster, or of all Ireland.

Cuchulain's Marriage

When the men of Ulster remembered Cuchulain's divine origin, they would fain have him married, so that he might not die childless; and for a year they searched all Erin for a fit bride for so great a champion. Cuchulain, however, went wooing for himself, to the dun of Forgall the Wily, a Druid of great power. Forgall had two daughters, of whom the younger, Emer, was the most lovely and virtuous maiden to be found in the country, and she became Cuchulain's chosen bride. Gallant was his wooing, and merry and jesting were her answers to his suit, for though Emer loved Cuchulain at first sight she would not accept him at once, and long they talked together. Finally Emer consented to wed Cuchulain when he had undergone certain trials and adventures for a year, and had accomplished certain feats, a test which she imposed on her lover, partly as a trial of his worthiness and constancy and partly to satisfy her father Forgall, who would not agree to the marriage. When Cuchulain returned triumphant at the end of the year, he rescued Emer from the confinement in which her father had placed her, and won her at the sword's point; they were wedded, and dwelt at Armagh, the capital of Ulster, under the protection of King Conor.

Bricriu's Feast

It happened that at Conor's court was one chief who delighted in making mischief, as Thersites among the Grecian leaders. This man, Bricriu of the Bitter Tongue, came to King Conor and invited him and all the heroes of the Red Branch, the royal bodyguard of Ulster, to a feast at his new dwelling, for he felt sure he could find some occasion to stir up strife at a feast. King Conor, however, and the Red Branch heroes, distrusted Bricriu so much that they refused to accept the invitation, unless Bricriu would give sureties that, having received his guests, he would leave the hall before the feasting began. Bricriu, who had expected some such condition, readily agreed, and before going home to prepare his feast took measures for stirring up strife among the heroes of Ulster.

Bricriu's Falsehood

Before Bricriu left Armagh he went to the mighty Laegaire and with many words of praise said: 'All good be with you, O Laegaire, winner of battles! Why should you not be Champion of Ireland for ever?'

'I can be, if I will,' said Laegaire.

'Follow my advice, and you shall be head of all the champions of Ireland,' said cunning Bricriu.

'What is your counsel?' said Laegaire.

'King Conor is coming to a feast in my house,' said Bricriu, 'and the Champion's Bit will be a splendid portion for any hero. That warrior who obtains it at this feast will be acclaimed Chief Champion of Erin. When the banquet begins do you bid your chariot-driver rise and claim the hero's portion for you, for you are indeed worthy of it, and I hope that you may get what you so well deserve!'

'Some men shall die if my right is taken from me,' quoth Laegaire; but Bricriu only laughed and turned away.

Bricriu Meets Conall Cearnach

Bricriu next met Conall Cearnach, Cuchulain's cousin, one of the chiefs of the Red Branch.

'May all good be with you, Conall the Victorious,' quoth he. 'You are our defence and shield, and no foe dare face you in battle. Why should you not be Chief Champion of Ulster?'

'It only depends on my will,' said Conall; and then Bricriu continued his flattery and insidious suggestions until he had stirred up Conall to command his charioteer to claim the Champion's Portion at Bricriu's feast. Very joyous was Bricriu, and very evilly he smiled as he turned away when he had roused the ambition of Conall Cearnach, for he revelled in the prospect of coming strife.

Bricriu Meets Cuchulain

'May all good be with you, Cuchulain,' said Bricriu, as he met the youthful hero. 'You are the chief defence of Erin, our bulwark against the foe, our joy and darling, the hero of Ulster, the favourite of all the maidens of Ireland, the greatest warrior of our land! We all live in safety under the protection of your mighty hand, so why should you not be the Chief Champion of Ulster? Why will you leave the Hero's Portion to some less worthy warrior?'

'By the god of my people, I will have it, or slay any bold man who dares to deprive me of it,' said Cuchulain.

Thereupon Bricriu left Cuchulain and travelled to his home, where he made his preparations for receiving the king, as if nothing were further from his thoughts than mischief-making and guile.

The Feast and the Quarrel

When King Conor and his court had entered Bricriu's house at Dundrum, and were sitting at the feast, Bricriu was forced by his sureties to leave the hall, for men feared his malicious tongue, and as he went to his watch-tower he turned and cried:

'The Champion's Portion at my feast is worth having; let it be given to the best hero in Ulster.'

The carving and distribution of the viands began, and when the Champion's Portion was brought forward it was claimed by three chariot-drivers, Laegaire's, Conall's, and Cuchulain's, each on behalf of his master; and when no decision was made by King Conor the three heroes claimed it, each for himself. But Laegaire and Conall united in defying Cuchulain and ridiculing his claim, and a great fight began in the hall, till all men shook for fear; and at last King Conor intervened, before any man had been wounded.

'Put up your swords,' he said. 'The Champion's Portion at this feast shall be divided among the three, and we will ask King Ailill and Queen Meave of Connaught to say who is the greatest champion.' This plan pleased every one but Bricriu, who saw his hopes of fomenting strife disappear.

The Women's Quarrel

Just at that moment the women rose and quitted the hall to breathe the fresh air, and Bricriu spied his opportunity. Going down from his watch-tower, he met Fedelm, the wife of Laegaire, with her fifty maidens and said to her:

'All good be with you to-night, Fedelm of the Fresh Heart! Truly in beauty, in birth, in dignity, no woman in Ulster is your equal. If you enter my hall first to-night, you will be queen of the Ulster women.'

Fedelm walked on merrily enough, but determined that she would soon re-enter the hall, and certainly before any other woman. Bricriu next met Lendabair the Favourite, Conall's wife, and gave her similar flattery and a similar prophecy, and Lendabair also determined to be first back at the house and first to enter the hall.

Then Bricriu waited till he saw Emer, Cuchulain's fair wife. 'Health be with you, Emer, wife of the best man in Ireland! As the sun outshines the stars, so do you outshine all other women! You should of right enter the house first, for whoever does so will be queen of the women of Ulster, and none has a better claim to be their queen than Cuchulain's wife, Forgall's fair daughter.'

The Husbands Intervene

The three fair women, each with her train of fifty maidens, watched one another carefully, and when one turned back towards the house the others accompanied her, step for step; and the noise of their returning footsteps as they raced along alarmed their husbands. Sencha, the king's wise counsellor, reassured them, saying, 'It is only a woman's quarrel; Bricriu has stirred up enmity among the wives of the heroes; and as he spoke Emer reached the hall, having suddenly outrun the others; but the doors were shut Then followed bitter complaints from Fedelm and Lendabair, both united against Emer, as their husbands had been against

Cuchulain. Again King Conor was forced to call for silence, since each hero was supporting his own wife's claims to be queen of the Ulster women. The strife was only calmed by the promise that the claim to the highest place should be settled by Ailill and Meave of Connaught, who would be impartial judges.

The Heroes Journey to Connaught

Bricriu's feast lasted for three days longer, and then King Conor and the Red Branch heroes returned to Armagh. There the dispute about the Championship began again, and Conor sent the heroes to Cruachan, in Connaught, to obtain a judgment from King Ailill. 'If he does not decide, go to Curoi of Munster, who is a just and wise man, and will find out the best hero by wizardry and enchantments.' When Conor had decided thus, Laegaire and Conall, after some disputation as to who should start first, had their chariots got ready and drove towards Cruachan, but Cuchulain stayed amusing himself and the women in Armagh. When his chariot-driver reproached him with losing the Champion's Portion through laziness Cuchulain replied: 'I never thought about it, but there is still time to win it. Yoke my steeds to the chariot.' By this time, however, the other two heroes were far, very far, in advance, with the chief men of Ulster following them.

Cuchulain's Steeds

Cuchulain had quite lately won two mighty magic steeds, which arose from two lonely lakes – the Grey of Macha, his best-beloved horse, and the Black Sainglend. The struggle between the hero and these magic steeds had been terrible before he had been able to tame them and reduce them to submission; now he had them yoked to his chariot, and when he had once started he soon came up with the other two heroes, and all three drove furiously towards Cruachan, with all the warriors of Ulster behind them.

Queen Meave Watches the Heroes

The noise of the advancing war-chariots reached Queen Meave at Cruachan, and she wondered greatly to hear thunder from a clear sky; but her fair daughter, looking from her window, said: 'Mother, I see chariots coming.'

'Who comes in the first?' asked Queen Meave.

'I see a big stout man, with reddish gold hair and long forked beard, dressed in purple with gold adornments; and his shield is bronze edged with gold; he bears a javelin in his hand.'

'That man I know well,' answered her mother. 'He is mighty Laegaire, the Storm of War, the Knife of Victory; he will slay us all, unless he comes in peace.'

'I see another chariot,' quoth the princess, 'bearing a fair man with long wavy hair, a man of clear red and white complexion, wearing a white vest and a cloak of blue and crimson. His shield is brown, with yellow bosses and a bronze edge.'

'That is valiant Conall the Victorious,' quoth Meave. 'Small chance shall we have if he comes in anger.'

'Yet a third chariot comes, wherein stands a dark, sad youth, most handsome of all the men of Erin; he wears a crimson tunic, brooched with gold, a long white linen cloak, and a white, gold-embroidered hood. His hair is black, his look draws love, his glance shoots fire, and the hero-light gleams around him. His shield is crimson, with a silver rim, and images of beasts shine on it in gold.'

Terror in Connaught

'Alas! that is the hero Cuchulain,' said Meave. 'He is more to be feared than all others. His voice in anger tells the doom of men; his wrath is fatal. Truly we are but dead if we have aroused Cuchulain's wrath.' After a pause: 'Tell me, daughter, are there yet other chariots?'

'The men of Ulster follow in chariots so numerous that the earth quakes beneath them, and their sound is as thunder, or the dashing waves of the sea.'

Now Queen Meave was terrified in good earnest, but hoped by a hearty welcome to turn aside the wrath of the heroes of Ulster; thus when they arrived at the dun of Cruachan they found the best of receptions, and all the Red Branch warriors were feasted for three days and nights.

Conor Explains the Matter

After three days Ailill of Connaught asked their business, and King Conor related to him everything as it had occurred – the feast, the dispute for the Champion's Portion, the women's quarrel, and the decision to be judged by King Ailill. This angered Ailill, who was a peaceable man.

'It was no friend of mine who referred you to me for I shall surely incur the hatred of two heroes,' quoth he.

'You are the best judge of all,' replied King Conor.

'Then I must have time – three days and nights – to decide,' said Ailill.

'We can spare our heroes so long,' quoth Conor, and therewith the Ulster men returned to Armagh, leaving the three claimants to the Championship at Cruachan.

The First Test

That night Ailill put them to an unexpected test. Their feast was served to them in a separate room, and the king went to his protectors, the Fairy People of the Hills, in the Good People's Hill at Cruachan, and begged some help in his judgment. They willingly aided him, and three magic beasts, in the shape of monstrous cats, were let into the room where the heroes feasted. When they saw them Laegaire and Conall rose up from their meal, clambered up among the rafters, and stayed there all night. Cuchulain waited till one attacked him, and then drawing his sword, struck the monster. It showed no further sign of fight, and Cuchulain kept watch all night, till the magic beasts disappeared at daybreak. When Ailill came into the room and saw the heroes as they had spent the night he laughed as he said:

'Are you not content to yield the Championship to Cuchulain?'

'Indeed no,' said Conall and Laegaire. 'We are are used to fighting men, not monstrous beasts.'

The Second Test

The next day King Ailill sent the heroes to his own foster-father, Ercol, to spend a night with him, that he also might test them. When they arrived, and had feasted, Laegaire was sent out that night to fight the witches of the valley. Fierce and terrible were these witches, and they beat Laegaire, and took his arms and armour.

When Conall went to fight them the witches beat him and took his spear, but he kept his sword and brought it back with honour. Cuchulain, who was the youngest, went last, and he too was being beaten, when the taunts of his chariot-driver, who was watching, aroused him, and he beat the witches, and bore off in triumph their cloaks of battle. Yet even after this the other two heroes would not acknowledge Cuchulain's superiority.

Ercol's Defeat

The next day Ercol fought with each champion separately, and conquered both Laegaire and Conall, terrifying the former so much that he fled to Cruachan and told Meave and Ailill that Ercol had killed the other two. When Cuchulain arrived, victorious, with Ercol tied captive at his chariot-wheels, he found all men mourning for him and Conall as for the dead.

Meave's Plan to Avoid Strife in Cruachan

Now indeed Ailill was in great perplexity, for he durst not delay his decision, and he dreaded the wrath of the two disappointed heroes. He and Queen Meave consulted long together, and at length Meave promised to relieve him of the responsibility of judgment. Summoning Laegaire to the king's room, she said:

'Welcome, O Laegaire! You are greatest of the warriors of Ulster. To you we give the headship of the heroes of Ireland and the Champion's Portion, and to your wife the right to walk first of all the women of Ulster. In token thereof we give you this cup of bronze with a silver bird embossed, to be seen by no man till you be come to King Conor in the Red Branch House at Armagh. Then show your cup and claim your right, and none will dispute it with you.'

So Laegaire went away well pleased, and they sent for Conall. To him they gave a silver cup, with a bird embossed in gold, and to him they pretended to adjudge the Championship, and Conall left them well content.

Cuchulain, who was playing chess, refused to attend the King of Connaught when he was summoned and Queen Meave had to entreat him to come to their private room. There they gave him a golden cup, with a bird designed in precious gems, with many words of flattery for Cuchulain and his fair and noble wife, Emer.

The Return of the Champions

Now the heroes, each well content, bade farewell to the court at Cruachan, and drove back to Armagh, but none durst ask how they had sped. That evening, at the banquet, when the Champion's Portion was set aside, Laegaire arose and claimed it, showing as proof that his claim was just the bronze cup he brought from Queen Meave.

But alas! Conall the Victorious had a silver cup, and while he was exulting in this proof of his rightful claim to the championship Cuchulain produced his golden cup, and the dispute began all over again. King Conor would have allowed Cuchulain's claim, but Laegaire vowed that his rival had bribed Ailill and Meave with great treasures to give him the golden cup, and neither Laegaire nor Conall would yield him the victory or accept the judgment as final. 'Then you must go to Curoi,' said the king, and to that they all agreed.

The Champions Visit Curoi

The next day the three champions drove to Kerry, where Curoi dwelt in a magic dun. He was away from home planning enchantments to test them, for he knew they were coming, but his wife welcomed them, and bade them watch the dun for one night each, beginning with Laegaire, as the eldest. Laegaire took up his sentinel's post outside the dun, and Curoi's wife worked the charm which prevented entrance after nightfall. The night was long and silent, and Laegaire thought he would have a quiet watch, when he saw a great shadow arise from the sea.

The Giant Fights Laegaire and Conall

This shadow took the shape of a huge giant, whose spears were mighty branch-stripped oaks, which he hurled at Laegaire. They did not touch him, however, and Laegaire made some show of fight; but the giant took him up, squeezed him so tightly as nearly to slay him, and then threw him over the magic wall of the dun, where the others found him lying half dead. All men thought that he had sprung with a mighty leap over the wall, since no other entrance was to be found, and Laegaire kept silence and did not explain to them.

Conall, who took the watch the second night, fared exactly as Laegaire had done, and likewise did not confess how he had been thrown over the wall of the dun, nor what became of the giant in the dawn.

Cuchulain's Trials

The third night was Cuchulain's watch, and he took his post outside the dun, and the gates and wall were secured by magic spells, so that none could enter. Vainly he watched till midnight, and then he thought he saw nine grey shadowy forms creeping towards him.

'Who goes there?' he cried. 'If you be friends, stop; if foes, come on!' Then the nine shadowy foes raised a shout, and fell upon the hero; but he fought hard and slew them, and beheaded them. A second and a third time similar groups of vague, shadowy foemen rushed at him, and he slew them all in like manner, and then, wearied out, sat down to rest.

The Dragon

Later on in the night, as he was still watching, he heard a heavy sound, like waves surging in the lake, and when he roused himself to see what it was he beheld a monstrous dragon. It was rising from the water and flying towards the dun, and seemed ready to devour everything in its way. When the dragon perceived him it soared swiftly into the air, and then gradually sank towards him, opening its terrible jaws. Cuchulain sprang up, giving his wonderful hero-leap, and thrust his arm into the dragon's mouth and down its throat; he found its heart, tore it out, and saw the monster fall dead on the ground. He then cut off its scaly head, which he added to those of his former enemies.

The Giant Worsted by Cuchulain

Towards daybreak, when feeling quite worn out and very sleepy, he became slowly aware of a great shadow coming to him westward from the sea. The shadow, as before, became a giant, who greeted him in a surly tone with, 'This is a bad night.' 'It will be worse yet for you,' said Cuchulain. The giant as he had done with the other heroes, threw oaks, but just missed him; and when he tried to grapple with him the hero leaped up with drawn sword. In his anger the hero-light shone round him, and he sprang as high as the giant's head, and gave him a stroke that brought him to his knees. 'Life for life, Cuchulain,' said the giant, and vanished at once, leaving no trace.

Cuchulain Re-enters the Dun

Now Cuchulain would gladly have returned to the fort to rest, but there seemed no way of entrance, and the hero was vexed at his own helplessness, for he thought his comrades had jumped over the magic walls. Twice he boldly essayed to leap the lofty wall, and twice he failed; then in his wrath his great strength came upon him, the hero-light shone round him, and he took a little run and, leaning on his spear, leaped so high and so far that he alighted in the middle of the court, just before the door of the hall.

   As he sighed heavily and wearily, Curoi's wife said: 'That is the sigh of a weary conqueror, not of a beaten man'; and Cuchulain went in and sat down to rest.

The Decision

The next morning Curoi's wife asked the champions: 'Are you content that the Championship should go to Cuchulain? I know by my magic skill what he has endured in the past night, and you must see that you are not equal to him.'

'The dragon sank towards him, opening its terrible jaws'

'Nay, that we will not allow,' quoth they. 'It was one of Cuchulain's friends among the People of the Hills who came to conquer us and to give him the Championship. We are not content, and we will not give up our claim, for the fight was not fair.'

'Go home now to Armagh, is Curoi's word and wait there until he himself brings his decision,' said Curoi's wife. So they bade her farewell, and went back to the Red Branch House in Armagh, with the dispute still unsettled; but they agreed to await peaceably Curoi's decision, and abide by it when he should bring it.

Uath, the Stranger

Some time after this, when Curoi had made no sign of giving judgment, it happened that all the Ulster heroes were in their places in the Red Branch House, except Cuchulain and his cousin Conall. As they sat in order of rank in the hall they saw a terrible stranger coming into the room. He was gigantic in stature, hideous of aspect, with ravening yellow eyes. He wore a skin roughly sewn together, and a grey cloak over it, and he sheltered himself from the light with a spreading tree torn up by the roots. In his hand he bore an enormous axe, with keen and shining edge. This hideous apparition strode up the hall and leant against a carved pillar beside the fire.

'Who are you?' asked one chieftain in sport. 'Are you come to be our candlestick, or would you burn the house down? Is this the place for such as you? Go farther down the hall!'

'My name is Uath, the Stranger, and for neither of those things am I come. I seek that which I cannot find in the whole world, and that is a man to keep the agreement he makes with me.'

The Agreement

'What is the agreement?' asked King Conor.

'Behold my axe!' quoth the stranger. 'The man who will grasp it to-day may cut my head off with it, provided that I may, in like manner, cut off his head to-morrow. Now you men of Ulster, heroes of the Red Branch, have won the palm through the wide world for courage, honour, strength, truth, and generosity; do you, therefore, find me a man to keep this agreement. King Conor is excepted, because of his royal dignity, but no other. And if you have no champion who dare face me, I will say that Ulster has lost her courage and is dishonoured.'

'It is not right for a whole province to be disgraced for lack of a man to keep his word,' said King Conor, 'but I fear we have no such champions here.'

Laegaire Accepts the Challenge

'By my word,' said Laegaire, who had listened attentively to the whole conversation, 'there will be a champion this very moment. Stoop down, fellow, and let me cut off your head, that you may take mine to-morrow.'

Then Uath chanted magic spells over the axe as he stroked the edge, and laid his neck on a block, and Laegaire hewed so hard that the axe severed the head from the body and struck deep into the block. Then the body of Uath arose, took up· the head and the axe, and strode away down the hall, all people shrinking out of its way, and so it passed out into the night.

'If this terrible stranger returns to-morrow he will slay us all,' they whispered, as they looked pityingly at Laegaire, who as trying in vain to show no signs of apprehension.

Laegaire and Conall Disgraced

When the next evening came and men sat in the Red Branch House, talking little and waiting for what would happen, in came Uath, the Stranger, as well and sound as before the terrible blow, bearing his axe, and eager to return the stroke. Alas! Laegaire's heart had failed him and he did not come, and the stranger jeered at the men of Ulster because their great champion durst not keep his agreement, nor face the blow he should receive in return for one he gave.

The men of Ulster were utterly ashamed, but Conall Cearnach, the Victorious, was present that night, and he made a new agreement with Uath. Conall gave a blow which beheaded Uath, but again, when the stranger returned whole and sound on the following evening, the champion was not to be found: Conall would not face the blow.

Cuchulain Accepts the Challenge

When Uath found that a second hero of Ulster had failed him he again taunted them all with cowardice and promise-breaking.

'What! is there not one man of courage among you Ulstermen? You would fain have a great name, but have no courage to earn it! Great heroes are you all! Not one among you has bravery enough to face me! Where is that childish youth Cuchulain! A poor miserable fellow he is, but I would like to see if his word is better to be relied on than the word of these two great heroes.'

'A youth I may be,' said Cuchulain, 'but I will keep my word without any agreement.'

Uath laughed aloud. 'Yes! that is likely, is it not? And you with so great a fear of death!'

Thereupon the youth leaped up, caught the deadly axe, severed the giant's head as he stood with one stroke.

Cuchulain Stands the Test

The next day the Red Branch heroes watched Cuchulain to see what he would do. The would not have been surprised if he had failed like the others, who now were present. The champion, however, showed no signs of failing or retreat. He sat sorrowfully in his place, waiting for the certain death that must come, and regretting his rashness, but with no thought of breaking his word.

With a sigh he said to King Conor as they waited: 'Do not leave this place till all

is over. Death is coming to me very surely, but I must fulfil my agreement, for I would rather die than break my word.'

Towards the close of day Uath strode into the hall, exultant.

'Where is Cuchulain?' he cried.

'Here I am,' was the reply.

'Ah, poor boy! your speech is sad to-night, and the fear of death lies heavy on you; but at least you have redeemed your word and have not failed me.'

The youth rose from his seat and went towards Uath, as he stood with the great axe ready, and knelt to receive the blow.

Curoi's Decision and Cuchulain's Victory

The hero of Ulster laid his head on the block; but Uath was not satisfied. 'Stretch out your neck better,' said he.

You are playing with me, to torment me,' said Cuchulain. 'Slay me now speedily, for I did not keep you waiting last night.'

However, he stretched out his neck as Uath bade, and the stranger raised his axe until it crashed upwards through the rafters of the hall, like the crash of trees falling in a storm. When the axe came down with a terrific sound all men looked fearfully at Cuchulain. The descending axe had not even touched him; it had come down with the blunt side on the ground, and the youth knelt there unharmed. Smiling at him, and leaning on his axe, stood no terrible and hideous stranger, but Curoi of Kerry, come to give his decision at last.

'Rise up, Cuchulain,' said Curoi. 'There is none among all the heroes of Ulster to equal you in courage and loyalty and truth. The Championship of the Heroes of Ireland is yours from this day forth, and the Champion's Portion at all feasts; and to your wife I adjudge the first place among all the women of Ulster. Woe to him who dares to dispute this decision! Thereupon Curoi vanished, and the Red Branch warriors gathered around Cuchulain, and all with one voice acclaimed him the Champion of the Heroes of all Ireland – a title which has clung to him until this day.

The Tale of Gamelyn

THE *Tale Of Gamelyn* is an anonymous romance dating from around 1350. It is thought to have been written in the area to the north of London (though Northumberland has also been claimed). It is probably best known to us today under another unexpected guise: it provides the essential plot-line for Shakespeare's *As You Like It*, via a sixteenth-century prose romance called *Rosalynde, or Euphues' Golden Legacy* by Thomas Lodge (1590). In this story the character of Gamelyn is named Rosader, the bad older brother Saladyne, and the good middle brother Fernandyne. The setting has moved from a medieval manor house north of London to the residence of a French Knight of Malta living in Bordeaux, though the story remains essentially the same. Shakespeare adapted this in his play, where Gamelyn becomes the exiled Duke, the usurping brother is named Frederick, and the good middle brother vanishes altogether.

No exact source for the original story is known, though key episodes can be identified from other works. The basic plot, which concerns the disinherited younger brother and his subsequent rise to fame and fortune, is not unlike both 'Havelok the Dane' and 'King Horn' though in other respects it is a very different tale. It can also be seen as a variant of the old faery-tale subject of the 'Wicked Elder Brothers' which appears in versions as ancient as that of Joseph and his brethren in biblical tradition.

But by far the most interesting link comes from a lasting association with the Robin Hood stories. It has even been suggested that in the episode where Gamelyn and his brother, Adam, flee to the greenwood we may have the prototype of the later accounts of Robin in Sherwood. However, this seems unlikely since Gamelyn, in the ballads where he appears, is generally described as an equal or even a rival to the Outlaw of Sherwood. In 'Robin and Gandelyn' (*sic*) he in fact avenges Robin's death, while in the later 'Robin Hood Newly Revived' he gets the better of Robin and is received into the outlaw band under the name Will Scarlet. Since Will has an older history than this the connection is undoubtedly a late one, but it shows that the 'Tale of Gamelyn' contributed to the growth of the Robin Hood myths, however obliquely.

The story also has a strong anti-clerical aspect, with the representatives of the Church being seen as corrupt and avaricious (see also 'Robin Hood') while the court officers, judge and jury are all seen in the worst possible light. While there are few literary associations for the court-room scenes, examples abound in legal history of corrupt magistrates and jurors being called to account. It is, indeed, the strong sense of justice, and the rights of the falsely accused hero, which dominate the story.

Interestingly, there is also evidence that Chaucer intended to rework the story as part of *The Canterbury Tales*, possibly as the unwritten 'Yeoman's Tale'. 'Gamelyn' thus appears in several manuscript copies of Chaucer's work, which has helped it to establish an ongoing readership.

The following extract, from the fourteenth-century original, gives a sense of the language of the time. I have modernized it for the sake of clarity, but have retained the caesura which breaks the lines in two, thus giving it a particular rhythm in keeping with the spirit of the original.

> Listen and hear   and hold your tongue
> And you shall hear talking   of Gamelyn the young.
> There was there announced   and cried a wrestling
> And therefore was set up   a ram and a ring
> And Gamelyn was mindful   to journey thereto
> For to prove his might   what he could do.
> 'Brother' said Gamelyn,   'By Saint Richard
> Thou must loan me tonight   a little fresh courser
> That is fresh to sport   on for to ride.
> I must on an errand   a little here beside.'
> 'By God' said his brother,   'of steeds in my stall
> Go and choose thee the best   and spare none of all
> Of steeds or of coursers   that stand there beside;
> And tell me good brother   whither thou wilt ride.'
> 'Here beside, brother,   is cried a wrestling
> And therefore shall be set up   a ram and a ring;
> Much worship it were,   brother, to us all,
> Might I the ram and ring   bring home to this hall.'

The Story

In the reign of King Edward I, there dwelt in Lincolnshire, near the vast expanse of the Fens, a noble gentleman, Sir John of the Marches. He was now old, but was still a model of all courtesy and a 'very perfect gentle knight.' He had three sons, of whom the youngest, Gamelyn, was born in his father's old age, and was greatly beloved by the old man; the other two were much older than he, and John, the eldest, had already developed a vicious and malignant character. Gamelyn and his second brother, Otho, reverenced their father, but John had no respect or obedience for the good gentleman, and was the chief trouble of his declining years, as Gamelyn was his chief joy.

The Father Feels His End Approaching

At last old age and weakness overcame the worthy old Sir John, and he was forced to take to his bed, where he lay sadly meditating on his children's future, and wondering how to divide his possessions justly among the three. There was no difficulty of inheritance or primogeniture, for all the knight's lands were held in fee-simple, and not in entail, so that he might bequeath them as he would. Sir John of the Marches, fearing lest he should commit an injustice, sent throughout the district for wise knights, begging them to come hastily, if they wished to see him alive, and help him. When the country squires and lords, his near neighbours, heard of his grave condition, they hurried to the castle, and gathered in the bedchamber, where the dying knight greeted them thus: 'Lords and gentlemen, I warn you in truth that I may no longer live; by the will of God death lays his hand upon me.' When they heard this they tried to encourage him, by bidding him remember that God can provide a remedy for every disease, and the good knight received their kindly words without dispute. 'That God can send remedy for an ill I will never deny; but I beseech you, for my sake, to divide my lands among my three sons. For the love of God deal justly, and forget not my youngest, Gamelyn. Seldom does any heir to an estate help his brothers after his father's death.'

How Shall He Dispose of His Estate

The friends whom Sir John had summoned deliberated long over the disposal of the estate. The majority wished to give all to the eldest son, but a strong minority urged the claims of the second, but all agreed that Gamelyn might wait till his eldest brother chose to give him a share of his father's lands. At last it was decided to divide the inheritance between the two elder sons, and the knights returned to the chamber where the brave old knight lay dying, and told him their decision. He summoned up strength enough to protest against their plan of distribution, and said:

> '"Nay, by St Martin, I can yet bequeath
> My lands to whom I wish: they still are mine.
> Then hearken, neighbours, while I make my will.
> To John, my eldest son, and heir, I leave

Five ploughlands, my dead father' heritage;
My second, Otho, ploughlands five shall hold,
Which my good right hand won in valiant strife;
All else I own, in lands and goods and wealth,
To Gamelyn, my youngest, I devise;
And I beseech you, for the love of God,
Forsake him not, but guard his helpless youth
And let him not be plundered of his wealth."'

Then Sir John, satisfied with having proclaimed his will, died with Christian resignation, leaving his little son Gamelyn in the power of the cruel eldest brother, now, in his turn, Sir John.

The Cruel Eldest Son

Since the boy was a minor, the new knight, as natural guardian, assumed the control of Gamelyn's land, vassals, education, and nurture; and full evilly he discharged his duties, for he clothed and fed him badly, and neglected his lands, so that his parks and houses, his farms and villages, fell into ruinous decay. The boy, when he grew older, noticed this and resented it, but did not realize the power in his own broad limbs and mighty sinews to redress his wrongs, though by the time he fully understood his injuries no man would dare to face him in fight when he was angry, so strong a youth had he become.

Gamelyn Resists

While Gamelyn, one day, walking in the hall, mused on the ruin of all his inheritance, Sir John came blustering in, and, seeing him, called out 'How now: is dinner ready?' Enraged at being addressed as if he were a mere servant, he replied angrily: 'Go and do your own baking; I am not your cook.'

Sir John almost doubted the evidence of his ears. 'What, my dear brother, is that the way to answer? Thou hast never addressed me so before!'

'No,' replied Gamelyn; 'until now I have never considered all the wrong you have done me. My parks are broken open, my deer are driven off; you have deprived me of my armour and my steeds; all that my father bequeathed to me is falling into ruin and decay. God's curse upon you, false brother!'

Sir John was now enraged beyond all measure, and shouted: 'Stand still, vagabond, and hold thy peace! What right hast thou to speak of land or vassals? Thou shalt learn to be grateful for food and raiment.'

'A curse upon him that calls me vagabond! I am no worse than yourself; I am the son of a lady and a good knight.'

Gamelyn Terrifies the Household

In spite of all his anger, Sir John was a cautious man, with a prudent regard for his own safety. He would not risk an encounter with Gamelyn, but summoned his servants and bade them beat him well, till he should learn better manners. But

'Go and do your own baking!'

when the boy understood his brother's intention he vowed that he would not be beaten alone – others should suffer too, and Sir John not the least. Thereupon, leaping on to the wall, he seized a pestle which lay there, and so boldly attacked the timid servants, though they were armed with staves, that he drove them in flight, and laid on furious strokes which quenched the small spark of courage in them. Sir John had not even that small amount of bravery: he fled to a loft and barred the door, while Gamelyn cleared the hall with his pestle, and scoffed at the cowardly grooms who fled so soon from the strife they had begun. When he sought for his brother he could not see him at first, but afterwards perceived his sorry countenance peeping from a window. 'Brother,' said Gamelyn, 'come a little nearer, and I will teach you how to play with staff and buckler.'

'Nay, by St Richard, I will not descend till thou hast put down that pestle. Brother, be no more enraged, and I will make peace with thee. I swear it by the grace of God!'

'I was forced to defend myself,' said Gamelyn, 'or your menials would have injured and degraded me: I could not let grooms beat a good knight's son; but now grant me one boon, and we shall soon be reconciled.'

Sir John's Guile

'Yes, certainly, brother; ask thy boon and I will grant it readily. But indeed I was only testing thee, for thou art so young that I doubted thy strength and manliness. It was only a pretence of beating that I meant.'

'This is my request,' said the boy: 'if there is to be peace between us you must surrender to me all that my father bequeathed me while he was alive.'

To this Sir John consented with apparent willingness, and even promised to repair the decayed mansions and restore the lands and farms to their former prosperity; but though he feigned content with the agreement and kissed his brother with outward affection yet he was inwardly meditating plans of treachery against the unsuspecting youth.

A Wrestling Match

Shortly after this quarrel between the brothers a wrestling competition was announced, the winner of which would become the owner of a fine ram and a ring of gold, and Gamelyn determined to try his powers. Accordingly he begged the loan of 'a little courser' from Sir John, who offered him his choice of all the steeds in the stable, and then curiously questioned him as to his errand. The lad explained that he wished to compete in the wrestling match, hoping to win honour by bearing away the prize; then, springing on the beautiful courser that was brought him ready saddled, he spurred his horse and rode away merrily, while the false Sir John locked the gate behind him, praying that he might get his neck broken in the contest. The boy rode along, rejoicing in his youth and strength, singing as he went, till he drew near the appointed place, and then he suddenly heard a man's voice lamenting aloud and crying, 'Wellaway! Alas!' and saw a venerable yeoman wringing his hands. 'Good man,' said Gamelyn, 'why art thou in such distress? Can no man help thee?'

A Dreaded Champion

'Alas!' said the yeoman. 'Woe to the day on which I was born! The champion wrestler here has overthrown my two stalwart sons, and unless God help them they must die of their grievous hurts. I would give ten pounds to find a man to avenge on him the injuries done to my dear sons.'

'Good man, hold my horse while my groom takes my coat and shoes, and I will try my luck and strength against this doughty champion.'

'Thank God!' said the yeoman. 'I will do it at once; I will guard thy coat and shoes and good steed safely – and may Jesus Christ speed thee well!'

Gamelyn Enters

When Gamelyn entered the ring, barefooted and stripped for wrestling, all men gazed curiously at the rash youth who dared to challenge the stalwart champion, and the great man himself, rising from the ground, strolled across to meet Gamelyn and said haughtily: 'Who is thy father, and what is thy name? Thou art, forsooth, a young fool to come here!'

Gamelyn answered equally haughtily: 'Thou knewest well my father while he lived: he was Sir John of the Marches, and I am his youngest son, Gamelyn.'

The champion replied: 'Boy, I knew thy father well in his lifetime, and I have heard of thee, and nothing good: thou hast always been in mischief.'

'Now I am older thou shalt know me better,' said Gamelyn.

Defeats the Champion

The wrestling had lasted till late in the evening, and the moon was shining on the scene when Gamelyn and the champion began their struggle. The wrestler tried many wily tricks, but the boy was ready for them all, and stood steady against all that his opponent could do. Then, in his turn, he took the offensive, grasped his adversary round the waist, and cast him so heavily to the ground that three ribs were broken, and his left arm. Then the victor said mockingly:

'Shall we count that a cast, or not reckon it?'

'By heaven! whether it be one or no, any man in thy hand will never thrive,' said the champion painfully.

The yeoman, who had watched the match with great anxiety, now broke out with blessings: 'Blessed be thou, young sir, that ever thou wert born!' and now taunting the fallen champion, said: 'It was young "Mischief" who taught thee this game.'

'He is master of us all,' said the champion. 'In all my years of wrestling I have never been mishandled so cruelly.'

Now the victor stood in the ring, ready for more wrestling, but no man would venture to compete with him, and the two judges who kept order and awarded the prizes bade him retire, for no other competitor could be found to face him.

But he was a little disappointed at this easy victory.

'Is the fair over? Why, I have not half sold my wares,' he said.

The champion was still capable of grim jesting. 'Now, as I value my life, any purchaser of your wares is a fool; you sell so dearly.'

'Not at all,' broke in the yeoman; 'you have bought your share full cheap, and made a good bargain.'

He Wins the Prizes

While this short conversation had been going on the judges had returned to their seats, and formally awarded the prize to Gamelyn, and now came to him, bearing the ram and the ring for his acceptance.

Gamelyn took them gladly, and went home the next morning, followed by a cheering crowd of admirers; but when the cowardly Sir John saw the people he bolted the castle doors against his more favourite and successful brother.

He Overcomes His Brother's Servants

The porter, obeying his master's commands, refused Gamelyn entrance; and the youth, enraged at this insult, broke down the door with one blow, caught the fleeing porter, and flung him down the well in the courtyard. His brother's servants fled from his anger, and the crowd that had accompanied him swarmed into courtyard and hall, while the knight took refuge in a little turret.

'Welcome to you all,' said Gamelyn. 'We will be masters here and ask no man's leave. Yesterday I left five tuns of wine in the cellar; we will drain them dry before you go. If my brother objects (as he well may, for he is a miser) I will be butler and caterer and manage the whole feast. Any person who dares to object may join the porter in the well.'

Naturally no objections were raised, and Gamelyn and his friends held high revel for a week, while Sir John lay hidden in his turret, terrified at the noise and revelry, and dreading what his brother might do to him now he had so great a following.

A Reckoning with Sir John

However, the guests departed quietly on the eighth day, leaving Gamelyn alone, and very sorrowful, in the hall where he had held high revel. As he stood there, musing sadly, he heard a timid footstep, and saw his brother creeping towards him. When he had attracted Gamelyn's attention he spoke out loudly: 'Who made thee so bold as to destroy all my household stores?'

'Nay, brother, be not wroth,' said the youth quietly. 'If I have used anything I have paid for it fully beforehand. For these sixteen years you have had full use and profit of fifteen good ploughlands which my father left me; you have also the use and increase of all my cattle and horses; and now all this past profit I abandon to you, in return for the expense of this feast of mine.'

Then said the treacherous Sir John: 'Hearken, my dear brother: I have no son, and thou shalt be my heir – I swear by the holy St John.'

'In faith,' said Gamelyn, 'if that be the case, and if this offer be made in all sincerity, may God reward you' for it was impossible for his generous disposition to suspect his brother of treachery and to fathom the wiles of a crafty nature; hence it happened that he was so soon and easily beguiled.

Gamelyn Allows Himself to be Chained

Sir John hesitated a moment, and then said doubtfully: 'There is one thing I must tell you, Gamelyn. When you threw my porter into the well I swore in my wrath that I would have you bound hand and foot. That is impossible now without your consent, and I must be forsworn unless you will let yourself be bound for a moment, as a mere form, just to save me from the sin of perjury.'

So sincere Sir John seemed, and so simple did the whole thing appear, that Gamelyn consented at once. 'Why, certainly, brother, you shall not be forsworn for my sake.' So he sat down and the servants bound him hand and foot; and then Sir John looked mockingly at him as he said: 'So now, my fine brother, I have you caught at last.' Then he bade them bring fetters and rivet them on Gamelyn's limbs, and chain him fast to a post in the centre of the hall. Then he was placed on his feet with his back to the post and his hands manacled behind him, and as he stood there the false brother told every person who entered that Gamelyn had suddenly gone mad, and was chained for safety's sake, lest he should do himself or others some deadly hurt. For two long days and nights he stood there bound, with no food or drink, and grew faint with hunger and weariness, for his fetters were so tight that he could not sit or lie down; bitterly he lamented the carelessness which made him fall such an easy prey to his treacherous brother's designs.

Adam Spencer to the Rescue

When all others had left the hall Gamelyn appealed to old Adam Spencer, the steward of the household, a loyal old servant who had known Sir John of the Marches, and had watched the boy grow up. 'Adam Spencer,' quoth he, 'unless my brother is minded to slay me, I am kept fasting too long. I beseech thee, for the great love my father bore thee, get the keys and release me from my bonds. I will share all my free land with thee if thou wilt help me in this distress.'

The poor old servant was greatly perplexed. He knew not how to reconcile his grateful loyalty to his dead master with the loyalty due to his present lord, and he said doubtfully: 'I have served thy brother for sixteen years, and if I release thee now he will rightly call me a traitor.'

'Ah, Adam! thou wilt find him a false rogue at the last, as I have done. Release me, dear friend Adam, and I will be true to my agreement, and will keep my covenant to share my land with thee.' By these earnest words the steward was persuaded, and, waiting till Sir John was safely in bed, managed to obtain possession of the keys and release Gamelyn, who stretched his arms and legs and thanked God for his liberty. 'Now,' said he, 'if I were but well fed no one in this house should bind me again to-night.' So Adam took him to a private room and set food before him; eagerly he ate and drank till his hunger was satisfied and he began to think of revenge. 'What is your advice, Adam? Shall I go to my brother and strike off his head? He well merits it.'

A Plan of Escape

'No,' answered Adam, 'I know a better plan than that. Sir John is to give a great feast on Sunday to many Churchmen and prelates; there will be present a great number of abbots and priors and other holy men. Do you stand as if bound by your post in the hall, and beseech them to release you. If they will be surety for you, your liberty will be gained with no blame to me; if they all refuse, you shall cast aside the unlocked chains, and you and I, with two good staves, can soon win your freedom. Christ's curse on him who fails his comrade!'

'Yes,' quoth Gamelyn, 'evil may I thrive if I fail in my part of the bargain. But if we must needs help them to do penance for their sins, you must warn me, brother Adam, when to begin.'

'By St Charity, master, I will give you good warning. When I wink at you be ready to cast away your fetters at once and come to me.'

'This is good advice of yours, Adam, and blessings on your head. If these haughty Churchmen refuse to be surety for me I will give them good strokes in payment.'

A Great Feast

Sunday came, and after Mass many guests thronged to the feast in the great hall; they all stared curiously at Gamelyn as he stood with his hands behind him, apparently chained to his post, and Sir John explained sadly that he, after slaying the porter and wasting the household stores, had gone mad, and was obliged to be chained, for his fury was dangerous. The servants carried dainty dishes round the table, and beakers of rich wines, but though Gamelyn cried aloud that he was fasting no food was brought to him. Then he spoke pitifully and humbly to the noble guests: 'Lords, for Christ's sake help a poor captive out of prison.' But the guests were hard-hearted, and answered cruelly, especially the abbots and priors, who had been deceived by Sir John's false tales. So harshly did they reply to the youth's humble petition that he grew angry. 'Oh,' said he, 'that is all the answer I am to have to my prayer! Now I see that I have no friends. Cursed be he that ever does good to abbot or prior!'

The Banquet Disturbed

Adam Spencer, busied about the removal of the cloth, looked anxiously at Gamelyn, and saw how angry he grew. He thought little more of his service, but, making a pretext to go to the pantry, brought two good oak staves, and stood them beside the hall door. Then he winked meaningly at Gamelyn, who with a sudden shout flung off his chains, rushed to the hall door, seized a staff, and began to lay about him lustily, whirling his weapon as lightly as if it had been a holy-water sprinkler. There was a dreadful commotion in the hall, for the portly Churchmen tried to escape, but the mere laymen loved Gamelyn, and drew aside to give him free play, so that he was able to scatter the prelates. Now he had no pity on these cruel Churchmen, as they had been without pity for him; he knocked them over, battered them, broke their arms and legs, and wrought terrible havoc among them; and during this time Adam Spencer kept the door so that none might escape. He called aloud to Gamelyn to respect the sanctity of men of Holy Church and shed no blood, but if he should by chance break arms and legs there would be no sacrilege, because no blood need be shed.

Sir John in Chains

Thus Gamelyn worked his will, laying hands on monks and friars, and sent them home wounded in carts and waggons, while some of them muttered: 'We were better at home, with mere bread and water, than here where we have had such a sorry feast!' Then Gamelyn turned his attention to his false brother, who had been unable to escape, seized him by the neck, broke his backbone with one blow from his staff, and thrust him, sitting, into the fetters that yet hung from the post where Gamelyn had stood. 'Sit there, brother, and cool thy blood,' said Gamelyn, as he and Adam sat down to a feast, at which the servants waited on them eagerly, partly from love and partly from fear.

The Sheriff's Men Appear

Now the sheriff happened to be only five miles away, and soon heard the news of this disturbance, and how Gamelyn and Adam had broken the king's peace; and, as his duty was, he determined to arrest the law-breakers. Twenty-four of his best men were sent to the castle to gain admittance and arrest Gamelyn and his steward; but the new porter, a devoted adherent of Gamelyn, denied them entrance till he knew their errand; when they refused to tell it, he sent a servant to rouse Gamelyn and warn him that the sheriff's men stood before the gate.

> 'Then answered Gamelyn: "Good porter, go;
> Delay my foes with fair speech at the gate
> Till I relieve thee with some cunning wile.
> If I o'erlive this strait, I will requite
> Thy truth and loyalty. Adam," quoth he,
> "Our foes are on us, and we have no friend –
> The sheriff's men surround us, and have sworn
> A mighty oath to take us: we must go
> Whither our safety calls us." He replied:
> "Go where thou wilt, I follow to the last
> Or die forlorn: but this proud sheriff's troop
> Will flee before our onset, to the fens."'

The Sheriff Arrives

As Gamelyn and Adam looked round for weapons the former saw a cart-staff, a stout post used for propping up the shafts; this he seized, and ran out at the little postern gate, followed by Adam with another staff. They caught the sheriff's twenty-four bold men in the rear, and when Gamelyn had felled three and Adam two, the rest took to their heels. 'What!' said Adam as they fled. 'Drink a draught of my good wine! I am steward here.' 'Nay,' they shouted back; 'such wine as yours scatters a man's brains far too thoroughly.' Now this little fray was hardly ended before the sheriff came in person with a great troop. Gamelyn knew not what to do, but Adam again had a plan ready. 'Let us stay no longer, but go to the greenwood: there we shall at least be at liberty.' The advice suited Gamelyn, and each drank a draught of wine, mounted his steed, and lightly rode away, leaving the empty nest for the sheriff, with no eggs therein. However, that officer dismounted, entered the hall, and found Sir John fettered and nearly dying. He released him, and summoned a leech, who healed his grievous wound, and enabled him to do more mischief.

Gamelyn Goes to the Greenwood

Meanwhile Adam wandered with Gamelyn in the greenwood, and found it very hard work, with little food. He complained aloud to his young lord:

> '"Would I were back in mine old stewardship –
> Full blithe were I, the leys to bear and keep!
> I like not this wild wood, with wounding thorns,
> And nought of food or drink, or restful ease."
> "Ah! Adam," answered Gamelyn, "in sooth
> Full many a good man's son feels bitter woe!
> Then cheer thee, Adam."'

As they spoke sadly together Gamelyn heard men's voices near by, and, looking through the bushes, saw seven score young men, sitting round a plentiful feast, spread on the green grass. He rejoiced greatly, bidding Adam remember that 'Boot cometh after bale,' and pointing out to him the abundance of provisions near at hand. Adam longed for a good meal, for they had found little to eat since they came to the greenwood. At that moment the master-outlaw saw them in the underwood, and bade his young men bring to him these new guests whom God had sent: perchance, he said, there were others besides these two. The seven bold youths who started up to do his will cried to the two new-comers: 'Yield and hand us your bows and arrows!' 'Much sorrow may he have who yields to you,' cried Gamelyn. 'Why, with five more ye would be only twelve and I could fight you all.' When the outlaws saw how boldly he bore himself they changed their tone, and said mildly: 'Come to our master, and tell him thy desire.' 'Who is your master?' quoth Gamelyn. 'He is the crowned king of the outlaws,' quoth they, and the two strangers were led away to the chief.

The master-outlaw, sitting on a rustic throne, with a crown of oak-leaves on his head, asked them their business, and Gamelyn replied: 'He must needs walk in the wood who may not walk in the town. We are hungry and faint, and will only shoot the deer for food, for we are hard bestead and in great danger.'

Gamelyn Joins the Outlaws

The outlaw leader had pity on their distress, and gave them food; and as they ate ravenously the outlaws whispered one to another: 'This is Gamelyn!' 'This is Gamelyn!' Understanding all the evils that had befallen him, their leader soon made Gamelyn his second in command; and when after three weeks the outlaw king was pardoned and allowed to return home, Gamelyn was chosen to succeed him and was crowned king of the outlaws. So he dwelt merrily in the forest, and troubled not himself about the world outside.

The Law at Work

Meanwhile the treacherous Sir John had recovered, and in due course had become sheriff, and indicted his brother for felony. As Gamelyn did not appear to answer the indictment he was proclaimed an outlaw and wolf's-head, and a price was set upon his life. Now his bondmen and vassals were grieved at this, for they feared the cruelty of the wicked sheriff; they therefore sent messengers to Gamelyn to tell him the ill news, and deprecate his wrath. The youth's anger rose at the tidings, and he promised to come and beard Sir John in his hall and protect his own tenants.

Gamelyn Arrested

It was certainly a stroke of rash daring thus to venture into the county where his brother was sheriff, but he strode boldly into the moot-hall, with his hood thrown back, so that all might recognize him, and cried aloud: 'God save all you lordings here present! But, thou broken-backed sheriff, evil mayst thou thrive! Why hast thou done me such wrong and disgrace as to have me indicted and proclaimed an outlaw?' Sir John did not hesitate to use his legal powers, but, seeing his brother was quite alone, had him arrested and cast into prison, whence it was his intention that only death should release him.

Otho as Surety

All these years the second brother, Otho, had lived quietly on his own lands and taken no heed of the quarrels of the two others; but now, when news came to him of Sir John's deadly hatred to their youngest brother, and Gamelyn's desperate plight, he was deeply grieved, roused himself from his peaceful life, and rode to see if he could help his brother. First he besought Sir John's mercy for the prisoner, for the sake of brotherhood and family love; but he only replied that Gamelyn must stay imprisoned till the justice should hold the next assize. Then Otho offered to be bail, if only his young brother might be released from his bonds and brought from the dismal dungeon where he lay. To this Sir John finally consented, warning Otho that if the accused failed to appear before the justice he himself must suffer the penalty for the breach of bail. 'I agree,' said Otho. 'Have him released at once, an deliver him to me.' Then Gamelyn was set free on his brother's surety, and the two rode home to Otho's house, talking sadly of all that had befallen, and how Gamelyn had become king of the outlaws. The next morning Gamelyn asked Otho's permission to go to the greenwood and see how his young men fared, but Otho pointed out so clearly how dreadful would be the consequences to him if he did not return that the young man vowed:

> '"I swear by James, the mighty saint of Spain,
> That I will not desert thee, nor will fail
> To stand my trial on the appointed day,
> If God Almighty give me strength and health
> And power to keep my vow. I will be there,
> That I may show what bitter hate Sir John,
> My cruel brother, holds against me."'

Gamelyn Goes to the Woods

Thereupon Otho bade him go. 'God shield thee from shame! Come when thou seest it is the right time, and save us both from blame and reproach.' So Gamelyn went gaily to the merry greenwood, and found his company of outlaws; and so much had they to tell of their work in his absence, and so much had he to relate of his adventures, that time slipped by, and he soon fell again into his former mode of life, and his custom of robbing none but Churchmen, fat abbots and priors, monks and canons, so that all others spoke good of him, and called him the 'courteous outlaw.'

The Term Expires

Gamelyn stood one day looking out over the woods and fields, and it suddenly came to his mind with a pang of self-reproach that he had forgotten his promise to Otho, and the day of the assize was very near. He called his young men (for he had learnt not to trust himself to the honour or loyalty of his brother the sheriff), and bade them prepare to accompany him to the place of assize, sending Adam on as a scout to learn tidings. Adam returned in great haste, bringing sad news. The judge was in his place, a jury empanelled to condemn Gamelyn to death, bribed thereto by the wicked sheriff, and Otho was fettered in the gaol in place of his brother. The news enraged Gamelyn, but Adam Spencer was even more infuriated; he would gladly have held the doors of the moot-hall and slain every person inside except Otho; but his master's sense of justice was too strong for that. 'Adam,' he said, 'we will not do so, but will slay the guilty and let the innocent escape. I myself will have some conversation with the justice in the hall; and meanwhile do ye, my men, hold the doors fast. I will make myself justice today, and thou, Adam shalt be my clerk. We will give sentence this day, and God speed our new work!' All his men applauded this speech and promised him obedience, and the troop of outlaws hastened to surround the hall.

Gamelyn in the Court

Once again Gamelyn strode into the moot-hall in the midst of his enemies, and was recognized by all. He released Otho, who said gently: 'Brother, thou hast nearly overstayed the time; the sentence has been given against me that I shall be hanged.'

'Brother,' said Gamelyn, 'this day shall thy foes and mine be hanged: the sheriff, the justice, and the wicked jurors.' Then Gamelyn turned to the judge, who sat as if paralysed in his seat of judgment, and said:

> '"Come from the seat of justice: all too oft
> Hast thou polluted law's clear stream with wrong;
> Too oft hast taken reward against the poor;
> Too oft has lent thine aid to villainy,
> And given judgment 'gainst the innocent.
> Come down and meet thine own meed at the bar,
> While I, in thy place, give more rightful doom
> And see that justice dwells in law for once."'

A Scene

The justice sat still, dumb with astonishment, and Gamelyn struck him fiercely, cut his cheek, and threw him over the bar so that his arm broke; and no man durst withstand the outlaw, for fear of his company standing at the doors. The youth sat down in the judge's seat, with Otho beside him, and Adam in the clerk's desk; and he placed in the dock the false sheriff, the justice, and the unjust jurors, and accused them of wrong and attempted murder. In order to keep up the forms of law, he empanelled a jury of his own young men, who brought in a verdict of 'Guilty,' and the prisoners were all condemned to death and hanged out of hand, though the false sheriff attempted to appeal to the brotherly affection of which he had shown so little.

Honour from the King

After this high-handed punishment of their enemies Gamelyn and his brother went to lay their case before King Edward, and he forgave them, in consideration of all the wrongs and injuries Gamelyn had suffered; and before they returned to their distant county the king made Otho sheriff of the county, and Gamelyn chief forester of all his free forests; his band of outlaws were all pardoned, and the king gave them posts according to their capabilities. Now Gamelyn and his brother settled down to a happy, peaceful life. Otho, having no son, made Gamelyn his heir, and the latter married a beauteous lady, and lived with her in joy till his life's end.

Black Colin of Loch Awe

N HIS original introduction to this story M. I. Ebbutt makes two interesting points. The first is that 'the only national heroes of Lowland Scotland are actual historical persons, with very little of the mythical character about them'. He goes on to list William Wallace, Robert the Bruce, Black Douglas, Andrew Barton, whose exploits 'are matter for serious chronicle and sober record rather than subject of tradition and myth'. Ebbutt's second point concerns the fact that the so-called 'mythical' heroes of Scotland, such as Finn and Oisin, in fact derive from Irish tradition, and that their stories were carried to the Western Isles and the Highlands by the tribes of Scots (Scotti) from Ireland. He therefore seeks in 'the private history of the country . . . to find a hero who will have something of the mythical in his story, something of the romance of the Middle Ages'.

Part, at least, of what Ebbutt says is true. There are no great national epics of the Scots, and most of their heroes are historical players in the long and frequently bloody history of that land. This certainly cannot be put down to the phlegmatic nature of the Scots, whose detailed and fascinating accounts of the faery folk have given us an astonishingly rich heritage. Rather it might be said that the description 'hero' was reserved for those who had lived and acted heroically, like those named above.

There is, however, a third strand of stories which in many ways comes closest to the idea of the hero myth. These are the lives of the Celtic saints, whose miraculous feats take us across the borders into the world of the supernatural and the magical.

In choosing to retell the story of Black Colin of Loch Awe, Ebbutt delved into the history of the clans, which certainly abounds in remarkable and powerful events. The origins of the Clan Campbell, of whom Black Colin is probably an historical member, are believed to derive their name from an ancient Gaelic nickname, 'Cam-beul' or 'Crooked Mouth'. They are descendants of Duncan mac Duibhne, a chieftain of Loch Awe who may well have been a relation of the Black Colin of the story. This same Duncan has been tentatively identified with one Siol Diarmuid who was himself the descendant of the great Fingalian hero Diarmuid o'Duibhne and who was, significantly, the son of Fergus 'Cerr-bel' or 'Wry mouth'. (They may also, interestingly enough, be related to the Celtic hero Arthur, the progenitor of the medieval king.)

Though it is virtually impossible to identify the Colin of the story, he may be the Sir Colin Campbell who was one of the twelve barons whose lands were joined to form the sheriffdom of Argyll in 1292. It is from this Colin Campbell of Loch Awe that the present chief, the Duke of Argyll, derived his Gaelic title 'Mac Cailein Mor', 'the Great Son of Colin', from which we may guess in what respect his name is held.

Sir Iain Moncreiffe of that Ilk, in his book on the Highland clans, adds this:

> The Campbells of Loch Awe originally lived in the island castle at Innischonaill in Loch Awe. They were distinguished by their loyalty to King Robert Bruce, whose sister married their then Chief, during the Scottish Wars of Independence. Throughout the Middle Ages they continued in their policy of loyalty to the Crown. When they moved from Loch Awe and the then 1st Earl of Argyll founded the burgh of Inveraray by Loch Fine in 1474, they continued this policy in a grander scale.

While there is no apparent record of a Colin Campbell having taken part in the Crusades, there is no doubt that a large number of Scottish knights made their way, via Rhodes, to the Holy Land, much as described in the story.

Though there is no particular text from which to quote in this example, I have thought it worth while to include a brief passage from another great Scottish poem, the style of which reflects the age if not the material. The poem in question is 'The Battle of Bannockburn' by John Barbour. The lines quoted here describe the battle in vivid detail.

Almighty God! Full valiantly
Sir Edward the Bruce and his men
Among them all demeaned them
To such good purpose
So hardy, worthy, and so fine
That their vanguard rushed was,
Because of which they left the place
And to the greater rout for company
They went, that then had on hand
So great employment, they were sore afraid,
For Scotts men them hard assayed,
That were in one great mass.
Who happened in that fight to fall,
I trow again he should not rise.
There man might see on every side
Great deeds achieved,
And many that mighty were and hardy
Down underfoot lay dead,
Where all the field of blood was red.
Armour and devices that they bore
With blood was so befouled there
That they might not described be.

The Knight of Loch Awe

During the wars between England and Scotland in the reigns of Edward I and Edward II one of the chief leaders in the cause of Scottish independence was Sir Nigel Campbell. The Knight of Loch Awe, as he was generally called, was a school-fellow and comrade of Sir William Wallace, and a loyal and devoted adherent of Robert Bruce. In return for his services in the war of independence Bruce rewarded him with lands belonging to the rebellious MacGregors, including Glenurchy, the great glen at the head of Loch Awe through which flows the river Orchy. It was a wild and lonely district and Sir Nigel Campbell had much conflict before he finally expelled the MacGregors and settled down peaceably in Glenurchy. There his son was born, and named Colin, and as years passed he won the nickname of Black Colin, from his swarthy complexion, or possibly from his character, which showed tokens of unusual fierceness and determination.

Black Colin's Youth

Sir Nigel Campbell, as all Highland chiefs did, sent his son to a farmer's family for fosterage. The boy became a child of his foster-family in every way; he lived on the plain food of the clansmen, oatmeal porridge and oatcake, milk from the cows, and beef from the herds; he ran and wrestled and hunted with his foster-brothers, and learnt woodcraft and warlike skill, broadsword play and the use of dirk and buckler, from his foster-father. More than all, he won a devoted following in the clan, for a man's foster-parents were almost dearer to him than his own father and mother, and his foster-brethren were bound to fight and die for him, and to regard him more than their own blood-relations. The foster-parents of Black Colin were a farmer and his wife, Patterson by name, living at Socach, in Glenurchy, and well and truly they fulfilled their trust.

He Goes on Crusade

In course of time Sir Nigel Campbell died, and Black Colin, his son, became Knight of Loch Awe, and lord of all Glenurchy and the country round. He was already noted for his strength and his dark complexion, which added to his beauty in the eyes of the maidens, and he soon found a lovely and loving bride. They dwelt on the Islet in Loch Awe, and were very happy for a short time, but Colin was always restless, because he would fain do great deeds of arms, and there was peace just then in the land.

At last one day a messenger arrived at the castle on the Islet bearing tidings that another crusade was on foot. This messenger was a palmer who had been in the Holy Land, and had seen all the holy places in Jerusalem. He told Black Colin how the Saracens ruled the country, and hindered men from worshipping at the sacred shrines; and he told how he had come home by Rome, where the Pope had just proclaimed another Holy War. The Pope had declared that his blessing would rest on the man who should leave wife and home and kinsfolk, and go forth to fight for the Lord against the infidel. As the palmer spoke Black Colin became greatly moved by his words, and when the old man had made an end he raised the hilt of his dirk and swore by the cross thereon that he would obey the summons and go on crusade.

The Lady of Loch Awe

Now Black Colin's wife was greatly grieved, and wept sorely, far she was but young and had been wedded no more than a year, and it seemed to her hard that she must be left alone. She asked her husband: 'How far will you go on this errand?' 'I will go as far as Jerusalem, if the Pope bids me, when I have come to Rome,' said he. 'Alas! and how long will you be away from me?' 'That I know not, but it may be for years if the heathen Saracens will not surrender the Holy Land to the warriors of the Cross.' 'What shall I do during those long, weary years?' asked she. 'Dear love, you shall dwell here on the Islet and be Lady of Glenurchy till I return again. The vassals and clansmen shall obey you in my stead, and the tenants shall pay you their rents and their dues, and in all things you shall hold my land for me.'

The Token

The Lady of Loch Awe sighed as she asked: 'But if you die away in that distant land how shall I know? What will become of me if at last such woeful tidings should be brought?'

'Wait for me seven years, dear wife,' said Colin, 'and if I do not return before the end of that time you may marry again and take a brave husband to guard your rights and rule the glen, for I shall be dead in the Holy Land.'

'That I will never do. I will be the Lady of Glenurchy till I die, or I will become the bride of Heaven and find peace for my sorrowing soul in a nunnery. No second husband shall wed me and hold your land. But give me now some token that we may share it between us; and you shall swear that on your deathbed you will send it to me; so shall I know indeed that you are no longer alive.'

'It shall be as you say,' answered Black Colin, and he went to the smith of the clan and bade him make a massive gold ring, on which Colin's name was engraved, as well as that of the Lady of Loch Awe. Then, breaking the ring in two, Colin gave to his wife the piece with his name and kept the other piece, vowing to wear it near his heart and only to part with it when he should be dying. In like manner she with bitter weeping swore to keep her half of the ring, and hung it on a chain round her neck; and so, with much grief and great mourning from the whole clan, Black Colin and his sturdy following of Campbell clansmen set out for the Holy Land.

The Journey

Sadly at first the little band marched away from all their friends and their homes; bagpipes played their loudest marching tunes, and plaids fluttered in the breeze, and the men marched gallantly, but with heavy hearts, for they knew not when they would return, and they feared to find supplanters in their homes when they came back after many years. Their courage rose, however, as the miles lengthened behind them, and by the time they had reached Edinburgh and had taken ship at Leith all was forgotten but the joy of fighting and the eager desire to see Rome and the Pope, the Holy Land and the Holy Sepulchre. Journeying up the Rhine, the Highland clansmen made their way through Switzerland and over the passes of the Alps down into the pleasant land of Italy, where the splendour of the cities surpassed their wildest imaginations; and so they came at last, with many other bands of Crusaders, to Rome.

The Crusade

At Rome the Knight of Loch Awe was so fortunate as to have an audience of the Pope himself, who was touched by the devotion which brought these stern warriors so far from their home. Black Colin knelt in reverence before the aged pontiff, whom he held in truth to be the Vicar of Christ on earth, and received his blessing, and commands to continue his journey to Rhodes, where the Knights of St John would give him opportunity to fight for the faith. The small band of Campbells went on to Rhodes, and there took service with the Knights, and won great praise from the Grand Master; but, though they fought the infidel, and exalted the standard of the Cross above the Crescent, Colin was still not at all satisfied. He left Rhodes after some years with a much-diminished band, and made his way as a pilgrim to Jerusalem. There he stayed until he had visited all the shrines in the Holy Land and prayed at every sacred spot. By this time the seven years of his proposed absence were ended, and he was still far from his home and the dear glen by Loch Awe.

The Lady's Suitor

While the seven years slowly passed away his sad and lonely wife dwelt in the castle on the Islet, ruling her lord's clan in all gentle ways, but fighting boldly when raiders came to plunder her clansmen. Yearly she claimed her husband's dues and watched that he was not defrauded of his rights. But though thus firm, she was the best help in trouble that her clan ever had, and all blessed the name of the Lady of Loch Awe.

So fair and gentle a lady, so beloved by her clan, was certain to have suitors if she were a widow, and even before the seven years had passed away there were men who would gladly have persuaded her that her husband was dead and that she was free. She, however, steadfastly refused to hear a word of another marriage, saying: 'When Colin parted from me he gave me two promises, one to return, if possible, within seven years, and the other to send me, on his deathbed, if he died away from me, a sure token of his death. I have not yet waited seven years, nor have I had the token of his death. I am still the wife of Black Colin of Loch Awe.'

This steadfastness gradually daunted her suitors and they left her alone, until but one remained, the Baron Niel MacCorquodale, whose lands bordered on Glenurchy, and who had long cast covetous eyes on the glen and its fair lady, and longed no less for the wealth she was reputed to possess than for the power this marriage would give him.

The Baron's Plot

When the seven years were over the Baron MacCorquodale sought the Lady of Loch Awe again, wooing her for his wife. Again she refused saying, 'Until I have the token of my husband's death I will be wife to no other man.' 'And what is this token, lady?' asked the Baron, for he thought he could send a false one. 'I will never tell that,' replied the lady. 'Do you dare to ask the most sacred secret between husband and wife? I shall know the token when it comes.' The Baron was not a little enraged that he could not discover the secret, but he determined to wed the lady and her wealth notwithstanding; accordingly he wrote by a sure and secret messenger to a friend in Rome, bidding him send a letter with news that Black Colin was assuredly dead, and that certain words (which the Baron dictated) had come from him.

A Forged Letter

One day the Lady of Loch Awe, looking out from her castle, saw the Baron coming, and with him a palmer whose face was bronzed by Eastern suns. She felt that the palmer would bring tidings, and welcomed the Baron with his companion. 'Lady, this palmer brings you sad news,' quoth the Baron. 'Let him tell it, then,' replied she, sick with fear. 'Alas! fair dame, if you were the wife of that gallant knight Colin of Loch Awe, you are now his widow,' said the palmer sadly, as he handed her a letter. 'What proof have you?' asked Black Colin's wife before she read the letter. 'Lady, I talked with the soldier who brought the tidings,' replied the stranger.

The letter was written from Rome to 'The Right Noble Dame the Lady of Loch Awe,' and told how news had come from Rhodes, brought by a man of Black Colin's band, that the Knight of Loch Awe had been mortally wounded in a fight against the Saracens. Dying, he had bidden his clansmen return to their lady, but they had all perished but one, fighting for vengeance against the infidels. This man, who had held the dying Knight tenderly upon his knee, said that Colin bade his wife farewell, bade her remember his injunction to wed again and find a protector, gasped out, 'Take her the token I promised; it is here,' and died; but the Saracens attacked the Christians again, drove them back, and plundered the bodies of the slain, and when the one survivor returned to search for the precious token there was none! The body was stripped of everything of value, and the clansman wound it in the plaid and buried it on the battlefield.

The Lady's Stratagem

There seemed no reason for the lady to doubt this news, and her grief was very real and sincere. She clad herself in mourning robes and bewailed her lost husband, but yet she was not entirely satisfied, for she still wore the broken half of the engraved ring on the chain round her neck, and still the promised death-token had not come. The Baron now pressed his suit with greater ardour than before, and the Lady of Loch Awe was hard put to it to find reasons for refusing him. It was necessary to keep him on good terms with the clan, for his lands bordered on those of Glenurchy, and he could have made war on the people in

Adam Bell writes the letter

the glen quite easily, while the knowledge that their chief was dead would have made them a broken clan. So the lady turned to guile, as did Penelope of old in similar distress. 'I will wed you, now that my Colin is dead,' she replied at last, 'but it cannot be immediately; I must first build a castle that will command the head of Glenurchy and of Loch Awe. The MacGregors knew the best place for a house, there on Innis Eoalan; there, where the ruins of MacGregor's White House now stand, will I build my castle. When it is finished the time of my mourning will be over, and I will fix the bridal day.' With this promise the Baron had perforce to be contented, and the castle began to rise slowly at the head of Loch Awe; but its progress was not rapid, because the lady secretly bade her men build feebly, and often the walls fell down, so that the new castle was very long in coming to completion.

Black Colin Hears the News

In the meantime all who loved Black Colin grieved to know that the Lady of Loch Awe would wed again, and his foster-mother sorrowed most of all, for she felt sure that her beloved Colin was not dead. The death-token had not been sent, and she sorely mistrusted the Baron MacCorquodale and doubted the truth of the palmer's message. At last, when the new castle was nearly finished and shone white in the rays of the sun, she called one of her sons and bade him journey to Rome to find the Knight of Loch Awe, if he were yet alive, and to bring sure tidings of his death if he were no longer living. The young Patterson set off secretly, and reached Rome in due course, and there he met Black Colin, just returned from Jerusalem. The Knight had at last realized that he had spent seven years away from his home, and that now, in spite of all his haste, he might reach Glenurchy too late to save his wife from a second marriage. He comforted himself, however, with the thought that the token was still safe with him, and that his wife would be loyal; great, therefore, was his horror when he met his foster-brother and heard how the news of his death had been brought to the glen. He heard also how his wife had reluctantly promised to marry the Baron MacCorquodale, and had delayed her wedding by stratagem, and he vowed that he would return to Glenurchy in time to spoil the plans of the wicked Baron.

Black Colin's Return

Travelling day and night, Black Colin, with his faithful clansman, came near to Glenurchy, and sent his follower on in advance to bring back news. The youth returned with tidings that the wedding had been fixed for the next day, since the castle was finished and no further excuse for delay could be made. Then Colin's anger was greatly roused, and he vowed that the Baron MacCorquodale, who had stooped to deceit and forgery to gain his ends, should pay dearly for his baseness. Bidding his young clansman show no sign of recognition when he appeared, the Knight of Loch Awe sent him to the farm in the glen, where the anxious foster-mother eagerly awaited the return of the wanderer. When she saw her son appear alone she was plunged into despair, for she concluded, not that Black Colin was dead, but that he would return too late. When he, in the beggar's disguise which he assumed, came down the glen he saw the smoke from the castle on the Islet, and said: 'I see smoke from my house, and it is the smoke of a wedding feast in preparation, but I pray God who sent us light and love that I may reap the fruit of the love that is there.'

The Foster-Mother's Recognition

The Knight then went to his foster-mother's house, knocked at the door, and humbly craved food and shelter as a beggar. 'Come in, good man,' quoth the mistress of the house; 'sit down in the chimney-corner, and you shall have your fill of oatcake and milk.' Colin sat down heavily, as if he were over-wearied, and the farmer's wife moved about slowly, putting before him what she had; and the Knight saw that she did not recognize him, and that she had been weeping quite recently. 'You are sad, I can see,' he said. 'What is the cause of your grief?' 'I am not minded to tell that to a wandering stranger,' she replied. 'Perhaps I can guess what it is,' he continued; 'you have lost some dear friend, I think.' 'My loss is great enough to give me grief,' she answered, weeping. 'I had a dear foster-son, who went oversea to fight the heathen. He was dearer to me than my own sons, and now news has come that he is dead in that foreign land. And the Lady of Loch Awe, who was his wife, is to wed another husband tomorrow. Long she waited for him, past the seven years he was to be away, and now she would not marry again, but that a letter has come to assure her of his death. Even yet she is fretting because she has not had the token he promised to send her; and she will only marry because she dare no longer delay.'

'What is this token?' asked Colin. 'That I know not: she has never told,' replied the foster-mother; 'but oh! if he were here Glenurchy would never fall under the power of Baron MacCorquodale.' 'Would you know Black Colin if you were to see him?' the beggar asked meaningly; and she replied: 'I think I should, for though he has been away for years, I nursed him, and he is my own dear fosterling.' 'Look well at me, then good mother of mine, for I am Colin of Loch Awe.'

The mistress of the farm seized the beggar-man by the arm, drew him out into the light, and looked earnestly into his face; then, with a scream of joy, she flung her arms around him, and cried: 'O Colin! Colin! my dear son, home again at last! Glad and glad I am to see you here in time! Weary have the years been since my nursling went away, but now you are home all will be well.' And she embraced him and kissed him and stroked his hair, and exclaimed at his bronzed hue and his ragged attire.

The Foster-Mother's Plan

At last Colin stopped her raptures. 'Tell me, mother, does my wife seem to wish for this marriage?' he asked; and his foster-mother answered: 'Nay, my son, she would not wed now but that, thinking you are dead, she fears the Baron's anger if she continues to refuse him. But if you doubt her heart, follow my counsel, and you shall be assured of her will in this matter.' 'What do you advise?' asked he. She answered: 'Stay this night with me here, and to-morrow go in your beggar's dress to the castle on the Islet. Stand with other beggars at the door, and refuse to

go until the bride herself shall bring you food and drink. Then you can put your token in the cup the Lady of Loch Awe will hand you, and by her behaviour you shall learn if her heart is in this marriage or not.' 'Dear mother, your plan is good, and I will follow it,' quoth Colin. 'This night I will rest here, and on the morrow I will seek my wife.'

The Beggar at the Wedding

Early next day Colin arose, clad himself in the disguise of a sturdy beggar, took a kindly farewell of his foster-mother, and made his way to the castle. Early as it was, all the servants were astir, and the whole place was in a bustle of preparation, while vagabonds of every description hung round the doors, begging for food and money in honour of the day. The new-comer acted much more boldly: he planted himself right in the open doorway and begged for food and drink in such a lordly tone that the servants were impressed by it, and one of them brought him what he asked – oatcake and buttermilk – and gave it to him, saying, 'Take this and begone.' Colin took the alms and drank the buttermilk, but put the cake into his wallet, and stood sturdily right in the doorway, so that the servants found it difficult to enter. Another servant came to him with more food and a horn of ale, saying, 'Now take this second gift of food and begone, for you are in our way here, and hinder us in our work.'

The Beggar's Demand

But he stood more firmly still, with his stout travelling-staff planted on the threshold, and said: 'I will not go.' Then a third servant approached, who said: 'Go at once, or it will be the worse for you. We have given you quite enough for one beggar. Leave quickly now, or you will get us into trouble.' The disguised Knight only replied: 'I will not go until the bride herself comes out to give me a drink of wine,' and he would not move, for all they could say. The servants at last grew so perplexed that they went to tell their mistress about this importunate beggar. She laughed as she said: 'It is not much for me to do on my last day in the old house,' and she bade a servant attend her to the door, bringing a large jug full of wine.

The Token

As the unhappy bride came out to the beggar-man he bent his head in greeting, and she noticed his travel-stained dress and said: 'You have come from far, good man'; and he replied: 'Yes, lady, I have seen many distant lands.' 'Alas others have gone to see distant lands and have not returned,' said she. 'If you would have a drink from the hands of the bride herself, I am she, and you may take your wine now'; and holding a bowl in her hands, she bade the servant fill it with wine, and then gave it to Colin. 'I drink to your happiness,' said he, and drained the bowl. As he gave it back to the lady he placed within it the token, the half of the engraved ring. 'I return it richer than I took it, lady,' said he, and his wife looked within and saw the token.

The Recognition

Trembling violently, she snatched the tiny bit of gold from the bottom of the bowl, which fell to the ground and broke at her feet, and then she saw her own name engraved upon it. She looked long and long at the token, and then, pulling a chain at her neck, drew out her half of the ring with Colin's name engraved on it. 'O stranger, tell me, is my husband dead?' she asked, grasping the beggar's arm. 'Dead?' he questioned, gazing tenderly at her; and at his tone she looked straight into his eyes and knew him. 'My husband!' was all that she could say, but she flung her arms around his neck and was clasped close to his heart. The servants stood bewildered, but in a moment their mistress had turned to them, saying, 'Run, summon all the household, bring them all, for this is my husband, Black Colin of Loch Awe come home to me again.' When all in the castle knew it there was great excitement and rejoicing, and they feasted bountifully, for the wedding banquet had been prepared.

The Baron's Flight

While the feast was in progress, and the happy wife sat by her long-lost husband and held his hand, as though she feared to let him leave her, a distant sound of bagpipes was heard, and the lady remembered that the Baron MacCorquodale would be coming for his wedding, which she had entirely forgotten in her joy. She laughed lightly to herself, and, beckoning a clansman, bade him go and tell the Baron that she would take no new husband, since her old one had come back to her, and that there would be questions to be answered when time served. The Baron MacCorquodale, in his wedding finery, with a great party of henchmen and vassals and pipers blowing a wedding march, had reached the mouth of the river which enters the side of Loch Awe; the party had crossed the river, and were ready to take boat across to the Islet, when they saw a solitary man rowing towards them with all speed. 'It is some messenger from my lady,' said the Baron, and he waited eagerly to hear the message. With dreadful consternation he listened to the unexpected words as the clansman delivered them, and then bade the pipers cease their music. 'We must return; there will be no wedding to-day, since Black Colin is home again,' quoth he; and the crestfallen party retraced their steps, quickening them more and more as they thought of the vengeance of the long-lost chieftain; but they reached their home in safety.

Castle Kilchurn

In the meantime Colin had much to tell his wife of his adventures, and to ask her of her life all these years. They told each other all, and Colin saw the false letter that had been sent to the Lady of Loch Awe, and guessed who had plotted this deceit. His anger grew against the bad man who had wrought this wrong and had so nearly gained his end, and he vowed that he would make the Baron dearly abide it. His wife calmed his fury somewhat by telling him how she had waited even beyond the seven years, and what stratagem she had used, and at last he promised not to make war on the Baron, but to punish him in other ways.

'Tell me what you have done with the rents of Glenurchy these seven years,' said he. Then the happy wife replied: 'With part I have lived, with part I have guarded the glen, and with part have I made a cairn of stones at the head of Loch Awe. Will you come with me and see it?' And Colin went, deeply puzzled. When they came to the head of Loch Awe, there stood the new castle, on the site of the old house of the MacGregors; and the proud wife laughed as she said: 'Do you like my cairn of stones? It has taken long to build.' Black Colin was much pleased with the beautiful castle she had raised for him, and renamed it Kilchurn Castle, which title it still keeps. True to his vow, he took no bloody vengeance on the Baron MacCorquodale, but when a few years after he fell into his power the Knight of Loch Awe forced him to resign a great part of his lands to be united with those of Glenurchy.

The Marriage of Sir Gawain

THIS story, which dates in its most complete form from the fourteenth century, is perhaps the best (though one of the least known) stories featuring the great Arthurian hero Gawain. It shows him to good advantage, displaying the qualities of chivalry and courtesy for which he was justly famed. It also forms the basis for Chaucer's 'Wife of Bath's Tale', in which form it is more familiar to students of medieval literature.

There is much within the story which bears comment. The attitude of the day which saw women as chattels, and linked them to their husbands as status symbols, is challenged throughout. Ragnall makes her own choice of husband, selecting Sir Gawain, the most famous and best-loved Knight of the Round Table, renowned for his courtesy and for his numerous relationships with women. Indeed, this service to all womankind gained him the reputation of a libertine, and as such he is portrayed in many of the later romances in which he appears. The reason for this seems to have been that as a Celtic hero Gawain (or as he is there known, Gwalchmai, the Hawk of May) was a champion of the Goddess and therefore of all women. To the disapproving minds of the medieval chroniclers and romancers this made him not only a pagan but also dangerous, and their reaction was to systematically blacken his name.

Ragnall herself is a fascinating character, independent and determined and possessed of an earthy sense of humour, despite her perilous situation. If either Arthur or Gawain had refused her offer she might have been condemned to perpetual ugliness, but her confidence in their chivalrous natures proves well founded. It is probable, from evidence found elsewhere, that she was, at one point, a faery woman, who sought to test the king and his nephew. As is often the way in such instances, the bride later vanishes, returning to faery after a number of years. In this version of the story she simply dies, having given birth to Gawain's son Guinglain.

The answer to the question: What is it women desire most? is here given as sovereignty. In the original text this is elaborated to mean more simply 'power over men', but as we have already seen in 'The Dream of Maxen Wledig', sovereignty is a far older figure, representing the land itself. No king in ancient Celtic tradition could lay claim to the rulership of the land until he had encountered her, sometimes being challenged to kiss or sleep with her in hideous form – at which point she turned into a beautiful woman, just as Ragnall does in the story given here.

In other versions of the story, particularly the ballad version found in Bishop Percy's *Reliques of Ancient English Poetry*, the cause of Ragnall's state and the giant's animosity towards Arthur is attributed to the arch-villainess of Arthurian tradition, Morgan le Fay. As a woman of faery blood herself and a lineal descendant of the Morrigan, she has a firmly grounded enmity with both Gawain and Arthur. In the most famous Gawain story, concerning his encounter with the Green Knight, she is again said to be the driving force behind the attack. Here she appears as a hideous old woman, while the Green Knight himself bears more than a little resemblance to the giant, who in most versions is called Gromer Somer Jour. That both these characters derive from more ancient ancestors than is apparent in the medieval poems is evident in both the works. In *Gawain and the Green Knight* the challenger bears a holly bough in his hand and dresses entirely in green, marking him out clearly enough as a type of Winter King. In Gromer's case, though his behaviour in the poem makes him no more than a challenger of a kind frequently encountered in Arthurian literature, his name suggests that he was once much more. Gromer Somer Jour may be translated as meaning 'Man of the Summer's Day', making him the polar opposite of the Green Knight, Summer Lord to the other's Winter King.

Behind both stories lies an ancient tale of the struggle of the kings of summer and winter for the hand of the Spring Maiden – here represented by Ragnall, who like her ancestor, Lady Sovereignty, represents the land in its barren, sleeping, wintry mode, which can be awoken to the beauty of spring by the love and trust of Gawain, himself a solar hero in Celtic tradition.

In most versions of the story Arthur encounters Gromer while out hunting. Here Ebbutt has chosen to include details of Arthur's quest on the lady's behalf, drawn from the ballad version, which adds a further twist to the events which are to follow. The extract from the original text which follows is from that same version, to be found in Bishop Percy's *Reliques of Ancient English Poetry*. It describes Arthur's meeting with Ragnall.

As rufully he rode over a moor,
    He saw a lady sat
Between an oak, and a green holly
    All clad in red scarlet.

Her nose was crooked, and turned outward,
    Her chin stood all awry;
And where there should have been her mouth,
    Lo! there was set her eye.

Her hair, like serpents, clung about,
    Her cheeks of deadly hew;
A worse formed lady than she was,
    No man might ever view.

Sir Gawayne

The true Knight of Courtesy is Sir Gawayne, King Arthur's nephew, who in many ways overshadows his more illustrious uncle. It is remarkable that the King Arthur of the mediaeval romances is either a mere ordinary conqueror or a secondary figure set in the background to heighten the achievements of his more warlike followers. The latter is the conception of Arthur which we find in this legend of the gentle and courteous Sir Gawayne.

King Arthur Keeps Christmas

One year the noble King Arthur was keeping his Christmas at Carlisle with great pomp and state. By his side sat his lovely Queen Guenever, the brightest and most beauteous bride that a king ever wedded, and about him were gathered the Knights of the Round Table. Never had a king assembled so goodly a company of valiant warriors as now sat in due order at the Round Table in the great hall of Carlisle Castle, and King Arthur's heart was filled with pride as he looked on his heroes. There sat Sir Lancelot, not yet the betrayer of his lord's honour and happiness, with Sir Bors and Sir Banier, there Sir Bedivere, loyal to King Arthur till death, there surly Sir Kay, the churlish steward of the king's household, and King Arthur's nephews, the young and gallant Sir Gareth, the gentle and courteous Sir Gawayne, and the false, gloomy Sir Mordred, who wrought King Arthur's overthrow. The knights and ladies were ranged in their fitting degrees and ranks, the servants and pages waited and carved and filled the golden goblets, and the minstrels sang to their harps lays of heroes of the olden time.

His Discontent

Yet in the midst of all this splendour the king was ill at ease, for he was a warlike knight and longed for some new adventure, and of late none had been known. Arthur sat moodily among his knights and drained the wine-cup in silence, and Queen Guenever, gazing at her husband, durst not interrupt his gloomy thoughts. At last the king raised his head, and, striking the table with his hand, exclaimed fiercely: 'Are all my knights sluggards or cowards, that none of them goes forth to seek adventures? You are better fitted to feast well in hall than fight well in field. Is my fame so greatly decayed that no man cares to ask for my help or my support against evildoers? I vow here, by the boar's head and by Our Lady, that I will not rise from this table till some adventure be undertaken.' 'Sire, your loyal knights have gathered round you to keep the holy Yuletide in your court,' replied Sir Lancelot; and Sir Gawayne said: 'Fair uncle, we are not cowards, but few evildoers dare to show themselves under your rule; hence it is that we seem idle. But see yonder! By my faith, now cometh an adventure.'

The Damsel's Request

Even as Sir Gawayne spoke a fair damsel rode into the hall, with flying hair and disordered dress, and, dismounting from her steed, knelt down sobbing at Arthur's feet. She cried aloud, so that all heard her: 'A boon, a boon, King Arthur! I beg a boon of you!' 'What is your request?' said the king, for the maiden was in great distress, and her tears filled his heart with pity. 'What would you have of me?' 'I cry for vengeance on a churlish knight, who has separated my love from me.' 'Tell your story quickly,' said King Arthur; and all the knights listened while the lady spoke.

'I was betrothed to a gallant knight,' she said, 'whom I loved dearly, and we were entirely happy until yesterday. Then as we rode out together planning our marriage we came, through the moorland ways, unnoticing, to a fair lake, Tarn Wathelan, where stood a great castle, with streamers flying, and banners waving in the wind. It seemed a strong and goodly place, but alas! it stood on magic ground, and within the enchanted circle of its shadow an evil spell fell on every knight who set foot therein. As my love and I looked idly at the mighty keep a horrible and churlish warrior, twice the size of mortal man, rushed forth in complete armour; grim and fierce-looking he was, armed with a huge club, and sternly he bade my knight leave me to him and go his way alone. Then my love drew his sword to defend me, but the evil spell had robbed him of all strength, and he could do nought against the giant's club; his sword fell from his feeble hand, and the churlish knight, seizing him, caused him to be flung into a dungeon. He then returned and sorely ill-treated me, though I prayed for mercy in the name of chivalry and of Mary Mother. At last, when he set me free and bade me go, I said I would come to King Arthur's court and beg a champion of might to avenge me, perhaps even the king himself. But the giant only laughed aloud. "Tell the foolish king," quoth he, "that here I stay his coming, and that no fear of him shall stop my working my will on all who come. Many knights have I in prison, some of them King Arthur's own true men; wherefore bid him fight with me, if he will win them back." Thus, laughing and jeering loudly at you, King Arthur, the churlish knight returned to his castle, and I rode to Carlisle as fast as I could.'

King Arthur's Vow

When the lady had ended her sorrowful tale all present were greatly moved with indignation and pity, but King Arthur felt the insult most deeply. He sprang to his feet in great wrath, and cried aloud: 'I vow by my knighthood, and by the Holy Rood, that I will go forth to find that proud giant, and will never leave him till I have overcome him.' The knights applauded their lord's vow, but Queen Guenever looked doubtfully at the king, for she had noticed the damsel's mention of magic, and she feared some evil adventure for her husband. The damsel stayed in Carlisle that night, and in the morning, after he had heard Mass, and bidden farewell to his wife, King Arthur rode away. It was a lonely journey to Tarn Wathelan, but the country was very beautiful, though wild and rugged, and the king soon saw the little lake gleaming clear and cold below him, while the enchanted castle towered up above the water, with banners flaunting defiantly in the wind.

The Fight

The king drew his sword Excalibur and blew a loud note on his bugle. Thrice his challenge note resounded, but brought no reply, and then he cried aloud: 'Come

forth, proud knight! King Arthur is here to punish you for your misdeeds! Come forth and fight bravely. If you are afraid, then come forth and yield yourself my thrall.'

The churlish giant darted out at the summons, brandishing his massive club, and rushed straight at King Arthur. The spell of the enchanted ground seized the king at that moment, and his hand sank down. Down fell his good sword Excalibur, down fell his shield, and he found himself ignominiously helpless in the presence of his enemy.

The Ransom

Now the giant cried aloud: 'Yield or fight, King Arthur; which will you do? If you fight I shall conquer you, for you have no power to resist me; you will be my prisoner, with no hope of ransom, will lose your land and spend your life in my dungeon with many other brave knights. If you yield I will hold you to ransom, but you must swear to accept the terms I shall offer.'

'What are they?' asked King Arthur. The giant replied: 'You must swear solemnly, by the Holy Rood, that you will return here on New Year's Day and bring me a true answer to the question, "What thing is it that all women most desire?" If you fail to bring the right answer your ransom is not paid, and you are yet my prisoner. Do you accept my terms?' The king had no alternative: so long as he stood on the enchanted ground his courage was overborne by the spell and he could only hold up his hand and swear by the Sacred Cross and by Our Lady that he would return, with such answers as he could obtain, on New Year's Day.

The King's Search

Ashamed and humiliated, the king rode away, but not back to Carlisle – he would not return home till he had fulfilled his task; so he rode east and west and north and south, and asked every woman and maid he met the question the churlish knight had put to him. "What is it all women most desire?" he asked, and all gave him different replies: some said riches, some splendour, some pomp and state; others declared that fine attire was women's chief delight, yet others voted for mirth or flattery, some declared that a handsome lover was the cherished wish of every woman's heart, and among them all the king grew quite bewildered. He wrote down all the answers he received, and sealed them with his own seal, to give to the churlish knight when he returned to the Castle of Tarn Wathelan; but in his own heart King Arthur felt that the true answer had not yet been given to him. He was sad as he turned and rode towards the giant's home on New Year's Day, for he feared to lose his liberty and lands, and the lonely journey seemed much more dreary than it had before, when he rode out from Carlisle so full of hope and courage and self-confidence.

The Loathly Lady

Arthur was riding mournfully through a lonely forest when he heard a woman's voice greeting him: 'God save you, King Arthur! God save and keep you!' and he turned at once to see the person who thus addressed him. He saw no one at all on his right hand, but as he turned to the other side he perceived a woman's form clothed in brilliant scarlet, the figure was seated between a holly-tree and an oak, and the berries of the former were not more vivid than her dress, and the brown leaves of the latter not more brown and wrinkled than her cheeks. At first sight King Arthur thought he must be bewitched – no such nightmare of a human face had ever seemed to him possible. Her nose was crooked and bent hideously to one side, while her chin seemed to bend to the opposite side of her face; her one eye was set deep under her beetling brow, and her mouth was nought but a gaping slit. Round this awful countenance hung snaky locks of ragged grey hair, and she was deadly pale, with a bleared and dimmed blue eye. The king nearly swooned when he saw this hideous sight, and was so amazed that he did not answer her salutation. The loathly lady seemed angered by the insult: 'Now Christ save you, King Arthur! Who are you to refuse to answer my greeting and take no heed of me? Little of courtesy have you and your knights in your fine court in Carlisle if you cannot return a lady's greeting. Yet, Sir King, proud as you are, it may be that I can help you, loathly though I be; but I will do nought for one who will not be courteous to me.'

The Lady's Secret

King Arthur was ashamed of his lack of courtesy, and tempted by the hint that here was a woman who could help him. 'Forgive me, lady,' said he; 'I was sorely troubled in mind, and thus, and not for want of courtesy, did I miss your greeting. You say that you can perhaps help me; if you would do this, lady, and teach me how to pay my ransom, I will grant anything you ask as a reward.' The deformed lady said: 'Swear to me, by Holy Rood, and by Mary Mother, that you will grant me whatever boon I ask, and I will help you to the secret. Yes, Sir King, I know by secret means that you seek the answer to the question, "What is it all women most desire?" Many women have given you many replies, but I alone, by my magic power, can give you the right answer. This secret I will tell you, and in truth it will pay your ransom, when you have sworn to keep faith with me.' 'Indeed, O grim lady, the oath I will take gladly,' said King Arthur, and when he had sworn it, with uplifted hand, the lady told him the secret, and he vowed with great bursts of laughter that this was indeed the right answer.

The Ransom

When the king had thoroughly realized the wisdom of the answer he rode on to the Castle of Tarn Wathelan, and blew his bugle three times. As it was New Year's Day, the churlish knight was ready for him, and rushed forth, club in hand, ready to do battle. 'Sir Knight,' said the king, 'I bring here writings containing answers to your question; they are replies that many women have given, and should be right;

'He hung his head and rode slowly away'

these I bring in ransom for my life and lands.' The churlish knight took the writings and read them one by one, and each one he flung aside, till all had been read, then he said to the king: 'You must yield yourself and your lands to me, King Arthur, and rest my prisoner; for though these answers be many and wise, not one is the true reply to my question; your ransom is not paid, and your life and all you have is forfeit to me.' 'Alas! Sir Knight,' quoth the king, 'stay your hand, and let me speak once more before I yield to you; it is not much to grant to one who risks life and kingdom and all. Give me leave to try one more reply.' To this the giant assented, and King Arthur continued: 'This morning as I rode through the forest I beheld a lady sitting, clad in scarlet, between an oak and a holly-tree; she says, "All women will have their own way, and this is their chief desire." Now confess that I have brought the true answer to your question, and that I am free, and have paid the ransom for my life and lands.'

The Price of the Ransom

The giant waxed furious with rage, and shouted: 'A curse upon that lady who told you this! It must have been my sister, for none but she knew the answer. Tell me, was she ugly and deformed?' When King Arthur replied that she was a loathly lady, the giant broke out: 'I vow to heaven that if I can once catch her I will burn her alive; for she has cheated me of being King of Britain. Go your ways, Arthur; you have not ransomed yourself, but the ransom is paid and you are free.'

Gladly the king rode back to the forest where the loathly lady awaited him, and stopped to greet her. 'I am free now, lady, thanks to you! What boon do you ask in reward for your help? I have promised to grant it you, whatever it may be.' 'This is my boon, King Arthur, that you will bring some young and courteous knight from your court in Carlisle to marry me, and he must be brave and handsome too. You have sworn to fulfil my request, and you cannot break your word.' These last words were spoken as the king shook his head and seemed on the point of refusing a request so unreasonable; but at this reminder he only hung his head and rode slowly away, while the unlovely lady watched him with a look of mingled pain and glee.

King Arthur's Return

On the second day of the new year King Arthur came home to Carlisle. Wearily he rode along and dismounted at the castle, and wearily he went into his hall, where sat Queen Guenever. She had been very anxious during her husband's absence, for she dreaded magic arts, but she greeted him gladly and said: 'Welcome, my dear lord and king, welcome home again! What anxiety I have endured for you! But now you are here all is well. What news do you bring, my liege ? Is the churlish knight conquered? Where have you had him hanged, and where is his head? Placed on a spike above some town-gate? Tell me your tidings, and we will rejoice together.' King Arthur only sighed heavily as he replied: 'Alas! I have boasted too much; the churlish knight was a giant who has conquered me, and set me free on conditions.' 'My lord, tell me how this has chanced.' 'His castle is an enchanted one, standing on enchanted ground, and surrounded with a circle of magic spells which sap the bravery from a warrior's mind and the strength from his arm. When I came on his land and felt the power of his mighty charms, I was unable to resist him, but fell into his power, and had to yield myself to him. He released me on condition that I would fulfil one thing which he bade me accomplish, and this I was enabled to do by the help of a loathly lady; but that help was dearly bought and I cannot pay the price myself.'

Sir Gawayne's Devotion

By this time Sir Gawayne, the king's favourite nephew, had entered the hall, and greeted his uncle warmly; then, with a few rapid questions, he learnt the king's news, and saw that he was in some distress. 'What have you paid the loathly lady for her secret, uncle?' he asked. 'Alas! I have paid her nothing; but I promised to grant her any boon she asked, and she has asked a thing impossible.' 'What is it?' asked Sir Gawayne. 'Since you have promised it, the promise must needs be kept. Can I help you to perform your vow?' 'Yes, you can, fair nephew Gawayne, but I will never ask you to do a thing so terrible,' said King Arthur. 'I am ready to do it, uncle, were it to wed the loathly lady herself.' 'That is what she asks, that a fair young knight should marry her. But she is too hideous and deformed; no man could make her his wife.' 'If that is all your grief,' replied Sir Gawayne, 'things shall soon be settled; I will wed this ill-favoured dame, and will be your ransom.' 'You know not what you offer,' answered the king. 'I never saw so deformed a being. Her speech is well enough, but her face is terrible, with crooked nose and chin, and she has only one eye.' 'She must be an ill-favoured maiden; but I heed it not,' said Sir Gawayne gallantly, 'so that I can save you from trouble and care.' 'Thanks, dear Gawayne, thanks a thousand times! Now through your devotion I can keep my word. To-morrow we must fetch your bride from her lonely lodging in the greenwood; but we will feign some pretext for the journey. I will summon a hunting party, with horse and hound and gallant riders, and none shall know that we go to bring home so ugly a bride.' 'Gramercy uncle,' said Sir Gawayne. 'Till to-morrow I am a free man.'

The Hunting Party

The next day King Arthur summoned all the court to go hunting in the green-wood close to Tarn Wathelan; but he did not lead the chase near the castle: the remembrance of his defeat and shame was too strong for him to wish to see the place again. They roused a noble stag and chased him far into the forest, where they lost him amid close thickets of holly and yew interspersed with oak copses and hazel bushes – bare were the hazels, and brown and withered the clinging oak leaves, but the holly looked cheery, with its fresh green leaves and scarlet berries. Though the chase had been fruitless, the train of knights laughed and talked gaily as they rode back through the forest, and the gayest of all was Sir Gawayne; he rode wildly down the forest drives, so recklessly that he drew level with Sir Kay, the churlish steward, who always preferred to ride alone. Sir Lancelot, Sir Stephen, Sir Banier, and Sir Bors all looked wonderingly at the reckless youth; but his younger brother, Gareth, was troubled, for he knew all was not well with

Gawayne, and Sir Tristram, buried in his love for Isolde, noticed nothing, but rode heedlessly, wrapped in sad musings.

Sir Kay and the Loathly Lady

Suddenly Sir Kay reined up his steed, amazed; his eye had caught the gleam of scarlet under the trees, and as he looked he became aware of a woman clad in a dress of finest scarlet, sitting between a holly-tree and an oak. 'Good greeting to you, Sir Kay,' said the lady, but the steward was too much amazed to answer. Such a face as that of the lady he had never even imagined, and he took no notice of her salutation. By this time the rest of the knights had joined him, and they all halted, looking in astonishment on the misshapen face of the poor creature before them. It seemed terrible that a woman's figure should be surmounted by such hideous features, and most of the knights were silent for pity's sake, but the steward soon recovered from his amazement, and his rude nature began to show itself. The king had not yet appeared, and Sir Kay began to jeer aloud. 'Now which of you would fain woo yon fair lady?' he asked. 'It takes a brave man, for methinks he will stand in fear of any kiss he may get, it must needs be such an awesome thing. But yet I know not, any man who would kiss this beauteous damsel may well miss the way to her mouth, and his fate is not quite so dreadful after all. Come, who will win a lovely bride!' Just then King Arthur rode up, and at sight of him Sir Kay was silent; but the loathly lady hid her face in her hands, and wept that he should pour such scorn upon her.

The Betrothal

Sir Gawayne was touched with compassion for this uncomely woman alone among these gallant and handsome knights, a woman so helpless and ill-favoured, and he said: 'Peace, churl Kay, the lady cannot help herself; and you are not so noble and courteous that you have the right to jeer at any maiden; such deeds do not become a knight of Arthur's Round Table. Besides, one of us knights here must wed this unfortunate lady.' 'Wed her?' shouted Kay. 'Gawayne, you are mad!' 'It is true, is it not, my liege?' asked Sir Gawayne, turning to the king; and Arthur reluctantly gave token of assent, saying, 'I promised her not long since, for the help she gave me in a great distress, that I would grant her any boon she craved, and she asked for a young and noble knight to be her husband. My royal word is given, and I will keep it; therefore have I brought you here to meet her.' Sir Kay burst out with, 'What? Ask me perchance to wed this foul quean? I'll none of her. Where'er I get my wife from, were it from the fiend himself, this hideous hag shall never be mine.' 'Peace, Sir Kay,' sternly said the king; 'you shall not abuse this poor lady as well as refuse her. Mend your speech, or you shall be knight of mine no longer.' Then he turned to the others and said: 'Who will wed this lady and help me to keep my royal pledge? You must not all refuse, for my promise is given, and for a little ugliness and deformity you shall not make me break my plighted word of honour.' As he spoke he watched them keenly, to see who would prove sufficiently devoted, but the knights all began to excuse themselves and to depart. They called their hounds, spurred their steeds, and pretended to search for the track of the lost stag again; but before they went Sir Gawayne cried aloud: 'Friends, cease your strife and debate, for I will wed this lady myself. Lady, will you have me for your husband?' Thus saying, he dismounted and knelt before her.

The Lady's Words

The poor lady had at first no words to tell her gratitude to Sir Gawayne, but when she had recovered a little she spoke: 'Alas! Sir Gawayne, I fear you do but jest. Will you wed with one so ugly and deformed as I? What sort of wife should I be for a knight so gay and gallant, so fair and comely as the king's own nephew? What will Queen Guenever and the ladies of the Court say when you return to Carlisle bringing with you such a bride? You will be shamed, and all through me.' Then she wept bitterly, and her weeping made her seem even more hideous; but King Arthur, who was watching the scene said: 'Lady, I would fain see that knight or dame who dares mock at my nephew's bride. I will take order that no such unknightly discourtesy is shown in my court,' and he glared angrily at Sir Kay and the others who had stayed, seeing that Sir Gawayne was prepared to sacrifice himself and therefore they were safe. The lady raised her head and looked keenly at Sir Gawayne, who took her hand, saying: 'Lady, I will be a true and loyal husband to you if you will have me; and I shall know how to guard my wife from insult. Come, lady, and my uncle will announce the betrothal.' Now the lady seemed to believe that Sir Gawayne was in earnest, and she sprang to her feet, saying: 'Thanks to you! A thousand thanks, Sir Gawayne, and blessings on your head! You shall never rue this wedding, and the courtesy you have shown. Wend we now to Carlisle.'

The Journey to Carlisle

A horse with a side-saddle had been brought for Sir Gawayne's bride, but when the lady moved it became evident that she was lame and halted in her walk, and there was a slight hunch on her shoulders. Both of these deformities showed little when she was seated, but as she moved the knights looked at one another, shrugged their shoulders and pitied Sir Gawayne, whose courtesy had bound him for life to so deformed a wife. Then the whole train rode away together, the bride between King Arthur and her betrothed, and all the knights whispering and sneering behind them. Great was the excitement in Carlisle to see that ugly dame, and greater still the bewilderment in the court when they were told that this loathly lady was Sir Gawayne's bride.

The Bridal

Only Queen Guenever understood, and she showed all courtesy to the deformed bride, and stood by her as her lady-of-honour when the wedding took place that evening, while King Arthur was groomsman to his nephew. When the long banquet was over, and bride and bridegroom no longer need sit side by side, the tables were cleared and the hall was prepared for a dance, and then men thought that Sir Gawayne would be free for a time to talk with his friends; but he refused. 'Bride and bridegroom must tread the first dance together, if she wishes it,' quoth he, and offered his lady his hand for the dance. 'I thank you, sweet husband,' said the grim lady as she took it and moved forward to open the dance with him; and through the long and stately measure that followed, so perfect was his dignity, and the courtesy and grace with which he danced, that no man dreamt of smiling as the deformed lady moved clumsily through the figures of the dance.

Sir Gawayne's Bride

At last the long evening was over, the last measure danced, the last wine-cup drained, the bride escorted to her chamber, the lights out, the guests separated in their rooms, and Gawayne was free to think of what he had done, and to consider how he had ruined his whole hope of happiness. He thought of his uncle's favour, of the poor lady's gratitude, of the blessing she had invoked upon him, and he determined to be gentle with her, though he could never love her as his wife. He entered the bride-chamber with the feeling of a man who has made up his mind to endure, and did not even look towards his bride, who sat awaiting him beside the fire. Choosing a chair, he sat down and looked sadly into the glowing embers and spoke no word.

'Have you no word for me, husband? Can you not even give me a glance?' asked the lady, and Sir Gawayne turned his eyes to her where she sat; and then he sprang up in amazement, for there sat no loathly lady, no ugly and deformed being, but a maiden young and lovely, with black eyes and long curls of dark hair, with beautiful face and tall and graceful figure. 'Who are you, maiden?' asked Sir Gawayne; and the fair one replied: 'I am your wife, whom you found between the oak and the holly-tree, and whom you wedded this night.'

Sir Gawayne's Choice

'But how has this marvel come to pass?' asked he, wondering, for the fair maiden was so lovely that he marvelled that he had not known her beauty even under that hideous disguise. 'It is an enchantment to which I am in bondage,' said she. 'I am not yet entirely free from it, but now for a time I may appear to you as I really am. Is my lord content with his loving bride?' asked she, with a little smile, as she rose and stood before him. 'Content!' he said, as he clasped her in his arms. 'I would not change my dear lady for the fairest dame in Arthur's court, not though she were Queen Guenever herself. I am the happiest knight that lives, for I thought to save my uncle and help a hapless lady, and I have won my own happiness thereby. Truly I shall never rue the day when I wedded you, dear heart.' Long they sat and talked together, and then Sir Gawayne grew weary, and would fain have slept, but his lady said: 'Husband, now a heavy choice awaits you. I am under the spell of an evil witch, who has given me my own face and form for half the day, and the hideous appearance in which you first saw me for the other half. Choose now whether you will have me fair by day and ugly by night, or hideous by day and beauteous by night. The choice is your own.'

The Dilemma

Sir Gawayne was no longer oppressed with sleep; the choice before him was too difficult. If the lady remained hideous by day he would have to endure the taunts of his fellows; if by night, he would be unhappy himself. If the lady were fair by day other men might woo her, and he himself would have no love for her; if she were fair to him alone, his love would make her look ridiculous before the court and the king. Nevertheless, acting on the spur of the moment, he spoke: 'Oh, be fair to me only – be your old self by day, and let me have my beauteous wife to myself alone.' 'Alas! is that your choice?' she asked. 'I only must be ugly when all are beautiful, I must be despised when all other ladies are admired; I am as fair as they, but I must seem foul to all men. Is this your love, Sir Gawayne?' and she turned from him and wept. Sir Gawayne was filled with pity and remorse when he heard her lament, and began to realize that he was studying his own pleasure rather than his lady's feelings, and his courtesy and gentleness again won the upper hand. 'Dear love, if you would rather that men should see you fair, I will choose that, though to me you will be always as you are now. Be fair before others and deformed to me alone, and men shall never know that the enchantment is not wholly removed.'

Sir Gawayne's Decision

Now the lady looked pleased for a moment, and then said gravely: 'Have you thought of the danger to which a young and lovely lady is exposed in the court? There are many false knights who would woo a fair dame, though her husband were the king's favourite nephew; and who can tell? – one of them might please me more than you. Sure I am that many will be sorry they refused to wed me when they see me to-morrow morn. You must risk my beauty under the guard of my virtue and wisdom, if you have me young and fair.' She looked merrily at Sir Gawayne as she spoke; but he considered seriously for a time, and then said: 'Nay, dear love, I will leave the matter to you and your own wisdom, for you are wiser in this matter than I. I remit this wholly unto you, to decide according to your will. I will rest content with whatsoever you resolve.'

The Lady's Story

Now the fair lady clapped her hands lightly, and said: 'Blessings on you, dear Gawayne, my own dear lord and husband! Now you have released me from the spell completely, and I shall always be as I am now, fair and young, till old age shall change my beauty as he doth that of all mortals. My father was a great duke of high renown who had but one son and one daughter, both of us dearly beloved, and both of goodly appearance. When I had come to an age to be married my father determined to take a new wife, and he wedded a witch-lady. She resolved to rid herself of his two children, and cast a spell upon us both, whereby I was transformed from a fair lady into the hideous monster whom you wedded, and my gallant young brother into the churlish giant who dwells at Tarn Wathelan. She condemned me to keep that awful shape until I married a young and courtly knight who would grant me all my will. You have done all this for me, and I shall be always your fond and faithful wife. My brother too is set free from the spell, and he will become again one of the truest and most gentle knights alive, though none can excel my own true knight, Sir Gawayne.'

The Surprise of the Knights

The next morning the knight and his bride descended to the great hall, where many knights and ladies awaited them, the former thinking scornfully of the hideous hag whom Gawayne had wedded, the latter pitying so young and gallant a knight, tied to a lady so ugly. But both scorn and pity vanished when all saw the bride. 'Who is this fair dame?' asked Sir Kay. 'Where have you left your ancient bride?' asked another, and all awaited the answer in great bewilderment. 'This is the lady to whom I was wedded yester evening,' replied Sir Gawayne. 'She was under an evil enchantment, which has vanished now that she has come under the power of a husband, and henceforth my fair wife will be one of the most beauteous ladies of King Arthur's court. Further, my lord King Arthur, this fair lady has assured me that the churlish knight of Tarn Wathelan, her brother, was also under a spell, which is now broken, and he will be once more a courteous and gallant knight, and the ground on which his fortress stands will have henceforth no magic power to quell the courage of any knight alive. Dear liege and uncle, when I wedded yesterday the loathly lady I thought only of your happiness, and in that way I have won my own lifelong bliss.'

King Arthur's joy at his nephew's fair hap was great, for he had grieved sorely over Gawayne's miserable fate, and Queen Guenever welcomed the fair maiden as warmly as she had the loathly lady, and the wedding feast was renewed with greater magnificence, as a fitting end to the Christmas festivities.

King Horn

'KING HORN' is probably the earliest truly 'English' romance to have survived, since it derives neither from Celtic nor French sources. It was written in a South Midlands dialect somewhere around 1225 by an unknown poet who seems to have been writing primarily for an audience of soldiers, farmers and townspeople, rather than the more courtly or chivalric readers or listeners.

Several attempts have been made to identify both the characters and the places mentioned with actual historical places and people. In the case of the former nothing has ever been successfully proven, while in the latter 'Suddene' may be either the Isle of Wight or Sussex, and 'Westernesse' is sometimes considered to be the Wirrall in Cheshire or an area of Cornwall.

The 'saracens' mentioned in the story are probably Vikings rather than Muslims, who never landed in any force on the English coast. In the poem they are indeed described as 'giants' which makes it more likely that the tall and powerful Northerners were meant, rather than the slighter, darker Easterners. In any case the lands and cultures are intended to be seen as more symbolic than actual.

The matter of the poem is largely traditional, deriving ultimately from numerous tales of orphaned royal children who fulfil a prophecy by avenging the death of their fathers and succeeding to the throne ('Havelok the Dane' and *Hamlet* are both of this type). The episode in which the young Childe Horn is set adrift in an open boat at the mercy of the waves, only to survive against all odds, is found in tales as far removed from each other as those of Herod and King Arthur.

Other famous elements include the magic ring given to Horn by Rymenhild, and the curious 'doubling' of episodes and names between the two women who love the hero, Rymenhild herself and Reynild. This whole part of the story may well have been influenced by the Tristan myth, in which the hero, again unable to marry the woman he loves (Iseult), marries another woman who bears the same name (Iseult White Hands). The fact that Horn also disguises himself with a blackened face (as does Tristan) may also derive from this source, since in the poem 'The Madness of Tristan' the hero does just this.

In addition there is a more than passing reference to the Odysseus story in the episode of the disguised Horn routing his true love's suitors. The popularity of this episode, which had Horn returning to interrupt the wedding feast and his subsequent recognition, is born out by the existence of the ballad of 'Hynd Horn' which survives in several versions and was still being sung in Scotland in the nineteenth century. The extracts from the ballad which follow give an idea of the way in which this aspect of the story caught the imagination.

> Hynd Horn fair and Hynd Horn free
> Where was you born and what country?
> In good greenwood where I was born,
> But my friends that have left me all forlorn.
>
> I gave my love a gay gold wand
> It was to rule o'er fair Scotland;
> And she gave to me a gay gold ring
> To me it had virtue above all thing . . .
>
> So he hoisted his sail and away went he,
> Away, away to some far country;
> But when he looked into his ring
> He knew that she loved no other man.
>
> So he hoisted his sail and home came he,
> Home, home again to his ain country;
> The first he met upon dry land
> It was an old old beggar man.
>
> What news, what news, ye old beggar man,
> What news, what news have you to give?
> No news, no news have I to give
> But the morn is our Queen's wedding day . . .

As in the story, Hynd Horn disguises himself in the beggar's clothes and makes his way to the wedding.

> So the bride came tripping down the stair
> With combs of yellow gold in her hair,
> With a glass of red wine in her hand
> To give to the old beggar man.
>
> Out of the glass he drank the wine,
> And into it he dropped the ring:

> O got you it by sea or got you it by land,
> Or got you it off a drowned man's hand?
>
> I got nae it by sea nor yet by land,
> Nor yet did I on a drowned man's hand;
> But I got it from you in my wooing gay,
> And I'll give it to you on your wedding day . . .

Again the bride recognizes the ring and all ends happily.

The symbolism of the ring, the horn and the fish caught in a net permeates the whole story, adding a mythic dimension to an otherwise prosaic tale. John Spiers, in his book *Medieval English Poetry* (London: Faber, 1971), suggests that the poem hides an original sun-god myth, citing Horn's radiance and his crossing of the sea to dispel the darkness of his adversaries as an indication of this. He goes on:

> The riddling play with the horn, the ring dropped into it and the allusion recalling the dream of the fish caught in the net are devices used to lead Rymenhild towards the eventual recognition. The connection between the name of the hero and the drinking horn is explicitly made in what is perhaps the most significant line in the poem – 'drink to Horn of horn'. As drinking horn, it is certainly related to the horn of plenty of the mythologies . . .

It is in such terms that we should see the story of King Horn. Not as a simple tale of adventure and courage, but as a fragment of a far older and more primal myth preserved within the texture of one of the earliest medieval romances which can be truly called part of the Matter of England.

The opening of the poem has a wonderful freshness which I have tried to convey in this modernized version.

> All be you well
> That listen to my song!
> A Song I shall you sing
> Of Murry the King.
> King he was of the West
> So long as he did last.
> Goodhild was his Queen
> No fairer might be seen.
> He had a son called Horn
> Fairer than he might never be born . . .
>
> He was white as a flower,
> Rose red was his colour,
> He was fair and bold
> And of fifteen winters old.
> In no kingdom
> Was his equal
> Twelve comrades he had
> All rich men's sons,
> And all were fair youths
> With him for to play . . .

The Royal Family of Suddene

There once lived and ruled in the pleasant land of Suddene a noble king named Murry, whose fair consort, Queen Godhild, was the most sweet and gentle lady alive, as the king was a pattern of all knightly virtues. This royal pair had but one child, a son, named Horn, now twelve years old, who had been surrounded from his birth with loyal service and true devotion. He had a band of twelve chosen companions with whom he shared sports and tasks, pleasures and griefs, and the little company grew up well trained in chivalrous exercises and qualities. Childe Horn had his favourites among the twelve. Athulf was his dearest friend, a loving and devoted companion; and next to him in Horn's affection stood Fikenhild, whose outward show of love covered his inward envy and hatred. In everything these two were Childe Horn's inseparable comrades, and it seemed that an equal bond of love united the three.

The Saracen Invasion

One day as King Murry was riding over the cliffs by the sea with only two knights in attendance he noticed some unwonted commotion in a little creek not far from where he was riding, and he at once turned his horse's head in that direction and galloped down to the shore. On his arrival in the small harbour he saw fifteen great ships of strange build, and their crews, Saracens all armed for war, had already landed, and were drawn up in warlike array. The odds against the king were terrible, but he rode boldly to the invaders and asked: 'What brings you strangers here? Why have you sought our land?' A Saracen leader, gigantic of stature, spoke for them all and replied: 'We are here to win this land to the law of Mahomet and to drive out the Christian law. We will slay all the inhabitants that believe on Christ. Thou thyself shalt be our first conquest, for thou shalt not leave this place alive.' Thereupon the Saracens attacked the little band, and though the three Christians fought valiantly they were soon slain. The Saracens then spread over the land, slaying, burning, and pillaging, and forcing all who loved their lives to renounce the Christian faith and become followers of Mahomet. When Queen Godhild heard of her husband's death and saw the ruin of her people she fled from her palace and all her friends and betook herself to a solitary cave, where she lived unknown and undiscovered, and continued her Christian worship while the land was overrun with pagans. Ever she prayed that God would protect her dear son, and bring him at last to his father's throne.

Horn's Escape

Soon after the king's death the Saracens had captured Childe Horn and his twelve comrades, and the boys were brought before the pagan emir. They would all have been slain at once or flayed alive, but for the beauty of Childe Horn, for whose sake their lives were spared. The old emir looked keenly at the lads, and said: 'Horn, thou art a bold and valiant youth, of great stature for thine age, and of full strength, yet I know thou hast not yet reached thy full growth. If we release thee with thy companions, in years to come we shall dearly rue it, for ye will become great champions of the Christian law and will slay many of us. Therefore ye must die.

But we will not slay you with our own hands, for ye are noble lads, and shall have one feeble chance for your lives. Ye shall be placed in a boat and driven out to sea, and if ye all are drowned we shall not grieve overmuch. Either ye must die or we, for I know we shall dearly abide your king's death if ye youths survive.' Thereupon the lads were all taken to the shore, and, weeping and lamenting, were thrust into a rudderless boat which was towed out to sea and left helpless.

Arrival at Westernesse

The other boys sat lamenting and bewailing their fate, but Childe Horn, looking round the boat, found a pair of oars, and as he saw that the boat was in the grasp of some strong current he rowed in the same direction, so that the boat soon drifted out of sight of land. The other lads were a dismal crew, for they thought their death was certain, but Horn toiled hard at his rowing all night, and with the dawn grew so weary that he rested for a little on his oars. When the rising sun made things clear, and he could see over the crests of the waves, he stood up in the boat and uttered a cry of joy. 'Comrades,' cried he, 'dear friends, I see land not far away. I hear the sweet songs of birds and see the soft green grass. We have come to some unknown land and have saved our lives.' Then Athulf took up the glad tidings and began to cheer the forlorn little crew, and under Horn's skilful guidance the little boat grounded gently and safely on the sands of Westernesse. The boys sprang on shore, all but Childe Horn having no thought of the past night and the journey; but he stood by the boat, looking sadly at it.

Farewell to the Boat

> '"Boat," quoth he, "which hast borne me on my way,
> Have thou good days beside a summer sea!
> May never wave prevail to sink thee deep!
> Go, little boat, and when thou comest home
> Greet well my mother, mournful Queen Godhild;
> Tell her, frail skiff, her dear son Horn is safe.
> Greet, too, the pagan lord, Mahomet's thrall,
> The bitter enemy of Jesus Christ,
> And bid him know that I am safe and well.
> Say I have reached a land beyond the sea,
> Whence, in God's own good time, I will return
> Then he shall feel my vengeance for my sire"'

Then sorrowfully he pushed the boat out into the ocean, and the ebbing tide bore it away, while Horn and his companions set their faces resolutely towards the town they could see in the distance.

King Ailmar and Childe Horn

As the little band were trudging wearily towards the town they saw a knight riding towards them, and when he came nearer they became aware that he must be some noble of high rank. When he halted and began to question them, Childe Horn recognized by his tone and bearing that this must be the king. So indeed it was, for King Ailmar of Westernesse was one of those noble rulers who see for themselves the state of their subjects and make their people happy by free, unrestrained intercourse with them. When the king saw the forlorn little company he said: 'Whence are ye, fair youths, so strong and comely of body? Never have I seen so goodly a company of thirteen youths in the realm of Westernesse. Tell me whence ye come, and what ye seek.' Childe Horn assumed the office of spokesman, for he was leader by birth, by courage, and by intellect. 'We are lads of noble families in Suddene, sons of Christians and of men of lofty station. Pagans have taken the land and slain our parents, and we boys fell into their hands. These heathen have slain and tortured many Christian men, but they had pity upon us, and put us into an old boat with no sail or rudder. So we drifted all night, until I saw your land at dawn, and our boat came to the shore. Now we are in your power, and you may do with us what you will, but I pray you to have pity on us and to feed us, that we may not perish utterly.'

Ailmar's Decision

King Ailmar was touched as greatly by the simple boldness of the spokesman as by the hapless plight of the little troop, and he answered, smiling: 'Thou shalt have nought but help and comfort, fair youth. But, I pray thee, tell me thy name.' Horn answered readily: 'King, may all good betide thee! I am named Horn, and I have come journeying in a boat on the sea – now I am here in thy land.' King Ailmar replied: 'Horn! That is a good name: mayst thou well enjoy it. Loud may this Horn sound over hill and dale till the blast of so mighty a Horn shall be heard in many lands from king to king, and its beauty and strength be known in many countries. Horn, come thou with me and be mine, for I love thee and will not forsake thee.'

Childe Horn at Court

The king rode home, and all the band of stranger youths followed him on foot, but for Horn he ordered a horse to be procured, so that the lad rode by his side; and thus they came back to the court. When they entered the hall he summoned his steward, a noble old knight named Athelbrus, and gave the lads in charge to him, saying, 'Steward, take these foundlings of mine, and train them well in the duties of pages, and later of squires. Take especial care with the training of Childe Horn, their chief; let him learn all thy knowledge of woodcraft and fishing, of hunting and hawking, of harping and singing; teach him how to carve before me, and to serve the cup solemnly at banquets; make him thy favourite pupil and train him to be a knight as good as thyself. His companions thou mayst put into other service, but Horn shall be my own page, and afterwards my squire.' Athelbrus obeyed the king's command, and the thirteen youths soon found themselves set to learn the duties of court life, and showed themselves apt scholars, especially Childe Horn, who did his best to satisfy the king and his steward on every point.

The Princess Rymenhild

When Childe Horn had been at court for six years, and was now a squire, he became known to all courtiers, and all men loved him for his gentle courtesy and his willingness to do any service. King Ailmar made no secret of the fact that Horn was his favourite squire, and the Princess Rymenhild, the king's fair daughter, loved him with all her heart. She was the heir to the throne, and no man had ever gainsaid her will, and now it seemed to her unreasonable that she should not be allowed to wed a good and gallant youth whom she loved. It was difficult for her to speak alone with him, for she had six maiden attendants who waited on her continually, and Horn was engaged with his duties either in the hall, among the knights, or waiting on the king. The difficulties only seemed to increase her love, and she grew pale and wan, and looked miserable. It seemed to her that if she waited longer her love would never be happy, and in her impatience she took a bold step.

Athelbrus Deceives the Princess

She kept her chamber, called a messenger, and said to him: 'Go quickly to Athelbrus the steward, and bid him come to me at once. Tell him to bring with him the squire Childe Horn, for I am lying ill in my room, and would be amused. Say I expect them quickly, for I am sad in mind, and have need of cheerful converse.' The messenger bowed, and, withdrawing, delivered the message exactly as he had received it to Athelbrus, who was much perplexed thereby. He wondered whence came this sudden illness, and what help Childe Horn could give. It was an unusual thing for the squire to be asked into a lady's bower, and still more so into that of a princess, and Athelbrus had already felt some suspicion as to the sentiments of the royal lady towards the gallant young squire. Considering all these things, the cautious steward deemed it safer not to expose young Horn to the risks that might arise from such an interview, and therefore induced Athulf to wait upon the princess and to endeavour to personate his more distinguished companion. The plan succeeded beyond expectation in the dimly lighted room, and the infatuated princess soon startled the unsuspecting squire by a warm and unreserved declaration of her affection. Recovering from his natural amazement, he modestly disclaimed a title to the royal favour and acknowledged his identity.

On discovering her mistake the princess was torn by conflicting emotions, but finally relieved the pressure of self-reproach and the confusion of maiden modesty by overwhelming the faithful steward with denunciation and upbraiding, until at last, in desperation, the poor man promised, against his better judgment, to bring about a meeting between his love-lorn mistress and the favoured squire.

Athelbrus Summons Horn

When Rymenhild understood that Athelbrus would fulfil her desire she was very glad and joyous; her sorrow was turned into happy expectation, and she looked kindly upon the old steward as she said: 'Go now quickly, and send him to me in the afternoon. The king will go to the wood for sport and pastime, and Horn can easily remain behind; then he can stay with me till my father returns at eve. No one will betray us; and when I have met my beloved I care not what men may say.'

Then the steward went down to the banqueting-hall, where he found Childe Horn fulfilling his duties as cup-bearer, pouring out and tasting the red wine in the king's golden goblet. King Ailmar asked many questions about his daughter's health, and when he learnt that her malady was much abated he rose in gladness from the table and summoned his courtiers to go with him into the greenwood. Athelbrus bade Horn tarry, and when the gay throng had passed from the hall the steward said gravely: 'Childe Horn, fair and courteous, my beloved pupil, go now to the bower of the Princess Rymenhild, and stay there to fulfil all her commands It may be thou shalt hear strange things, but keep rash and bold words in thy heart, and let them not be upon thy tongue. Horn, dear lad, be true and loyal now, and thou shalt never repent it.'

Horn and Rymenhild

Horn listened to this unusual speech with great astonishment, but, since Sir Athelbrus spoke so solemnly, he laid all his words to heart, and thus, marvelling greatly, departed to the royal bower. When he had knocked at the door, and had been bidden to come in, entering, he found Rymenhild sitting in a great chair, intently regarding him as he came into the room. He knelt down to make obeisance to her, and kissed her hand, saying, 'Sweet be thy life and soft thy slumbers, fair Princess Rymenhild! Well may it be with thy gentle ladies of honour! I am here at thy command, lady, for Sir Athelbrus the steward, bade me come to speak with thee. Tell me thy will, and I will fulfil all thy desires.' She arose from her seat, and, bending towards him as he knelt, took him by the hand and lifted him up, saying, 'Arise and sit beside me, Childe Horn, and we will drink this cup of wine together.' In great astonishment the youth did as the princess bade, and sat beside her and soon to his utter amazement, Rymenhild avowed her love for him, and offered him her hand. 'Have pity on me, Horn, and plight me thy troth, for in very truth I love thee, and have loved thee long, and if thou wilt I will be thy wife.'

Horn Refuses the Princess

Now Horn was in evil case, for he saw full well in what danger he would place the princess, Sir Athelbrus, and himself if he accepted the proffer of her lover. He knew the reason of the steward's warning, and tried to think what he might say to satisfy the princess and yet not be disloyal to the king. At last he replied: 'Christ save and keep thee, my lady Rymenhild, and give thee joy of thy husband, whosoever he may be! I am too lowly born to be worthy of such a wife; I am a mere foundling, living on thy father's bounty. It is not in the course of nature that such as I should wed a king's daughter, for there can be no equal match between a princess and a landless squire.'

Rymenhild was so disheartened and ashamed at this reply to her loving appeal that her colour changed, she turned deadly pale, began to sigh, flung her arms out wildly and fell down in a swoon. Chide Horn lifted her up, full of pity for her deep distress, and began to comfort her and try to revive her. As he held her in his arms he kissed her often and said:

'"Lady, dear love, take comfort and be strong!
For I will yield me wholly to thy guidance
If thou wilt compass one great thing for me.
Plead with King Ailmar that he dub me knight,
That I may prove me worthy of thy love.
Soon shall my knighthood be no idle dream,
And I will strive to do thy will, dear heart."'

Now at these words Rymenhild awoke from her swoon, and made him repeat his promise. She said: 'Ah! Horn, that shall speedily be done. Ere the week is past thou shalt be Sir Horn, for my father loves thee, and will grant the dignity most willingly to one so dear to him. Go now quickly to Sir Athelbrus, give him as a token of my gratitude this golden goblet and this ring; pray him that he persuade the king to dub thee knight. I will repay him with rich rewards for his gentle courtesy to me. May Christ help him to speed thee in thy desires!' Horn then took leave of Rymenhild with great affection, and found Athelbrus, to whom he delivered the gift and the princess's message, which the steward received with due reverence.

Horn Becomes a Knight

This plan seemed to Athelbrus very good, for it raised Horn to be a member of the noble Order of Knights, and would give him other chances of distinguishing himself. Accordingly he went to the king as he sat over the evening meal, and spoke thus: 'Sir King, hear my words, for I have counsel for thee. To-morrow is the festival of thy birth, and the whole realm of Westernesse must rejoice in its master's joy. Wear thou thy crown in solemn state, and I think it were nought amiss if thou shouldst knight young Horn, who will become a worthy defender of thy throne.' 'That were well done,' said King Ailmar. 'The youth pleases me, and I will knight him with my own sword. Afterwards he shall knight his twelve comrades the same day.'

The next day the ceremony of knighting was performed with all solemnity, and at its close a great banquet was prepared and all men made merry. But Princess Rymenhild was somewhat sad. She could not descend to the hall and take her customary place, for this was a feast for knights alone, and she would not be without her betrothed one moment longer, so she sent a messenger to fetch Sir Horn to her bower.

Horn and Athulf Go to Rymenhild

Now that Horn was a newly dubbed knight he would not allow the slightest shadow of dishonour to cloud his conduct; accordingly, when he obeyed Rymenhild's summons he was accompanied by Athulf. 'Welcome, Sir Horn and Sir Athulf,' she cried, holding out her hands in greeting. 'Love, now that thou hast thy will, keep thy plighted word and make me thy wife; release me from my anxiety and do as thou hast said.'

'"Dear Rymenhild, hold thou thyself at peace,"
Quoth young Sir Horn; "I will perform my vow.
But first I must ride forth to prove my might;

Must conquer hardships, and my own worse self,
Ere I can hope to woo and wed my bride.
We are but new-fledged knights of one day's growth,
And yet we know the custom of our state
Is first to fight and win a hero's name,
Then afterwards to win a lady's heart.
This day will I do bravely for thy love
And show my valour and deep devotion
In prowess 'gainst the foes of this thy land
If I come back in peace, I claim my wife."'

Rymenhild protested no longer, for she saw that where honour was concerned Horn was inflexible. 'My true knight,' said she, 'I must in sooth believe thee, and I feel that I may. Take this ring engraved with my name, wrought by the most skilled worker of our court, and wear it always, for it has magic virtues. The gems are of such saving power that thou shalt fear no strokes in battle, nor ever be cast down if thou gaze on this ring and think of thy love. Athulf, too, shall have a similar ring. And now, Horn, I commend thee to God, and may Christ give thee good success and bring thee back in safety!'

Horn's First Exploit

After taking an affectionate farewell of Rymenhild, Horn went down to the hall, and, seeing all the other new-made knights going in to the banquet, he slipped quietly away and betook himself to the stables. There he armed himself secretly and mounted his white charger, which pranced and reared joyfully as he rode away; and Horn began to sing for joy of heart, for he had won his chief desire, and was happy in the love of the king's daughter. As he rode by the shore he saw a stranger ship drawn up on the beach, and recognized the banner and accoutrements of her Saracen crew, for he had never forgotten the heathens who had slain his father. 'What brings you here?' he asked angrily, and as fearlessly as King Murry had done, and received the same answer: 'We will conquer this land and slay the inhabitants.' Then Horn's anger rose, he gripped his sword, and rushed boldly at the heathens, and slew many of them, striking off a head at each blow. The onslaught was so sudden that the Saracens were taken by surprise at first, but then they rallied and surrounded Horn, so that matters began to look dangerous for him. Then he remembered the betrothal ring, and looked on it, thinking earnestly of Rymenhild, his dear love, and such courage came to him that he was able to defeat the pagans and slay their leader. The others, sorely wounded – for none escaped unhurt – hurried on board ship and put to sea, and Horn, bearing the Saracen leader's head on his sword's point, rode back to the royal palace. Here he related to King Ailmar this first exploit of his knighthood and presented the head of the foe to the king, who rejoiced greatly at Horn's valour and success.

Rymenhild's Dream

The next day the king and all the court rode out hunting, but Horn made an excuse to stay behind with the princess, and the false and wily Fikenhild was also left at

Horn kills the Saracen Leader

home, and he crept secretly to Rymenhild's bower to spy on her. She was sitting weeping bitterly when Sir Horn entered. He was amazed. 'Love, for mercy's sake, why weepest thou so sorely?' he asked; and she replied: 'I have had a mournful dream. I dreamt that I was casting a net and had caught a great fish, which began to burst the net. I greatly fear that I shall lose my chosen fish.' Then she looked sadly at Horn. But the young knight was in a cheery mood, and replied: 'May Christ and St Stephen turn thy dream to good! If I am thy fish, I will never deceive thee nor do aught to displease thee, and hereto I plight thee my troth. But I would rather interpret thy dream otherwise. This great fish which burst thy net is some one who wishes us ill, and will do us harm soon.' Yet in spite of Horn's brave words it was a sad betrothal, for Rymenhild wept bitterly, and her lover could not stop her tears.

Fikenhild's False Accusation

Fikenhild had listened to all their conversation with growing envy and anger, and now he stole away silently, and met King Ailmar returning from the chase.

> '"King Ailmar," said the false one, "see I bring
> A needed warning, that thou guard thyself,
> For Horn will take they life; I heard him vow
> To slay thee, or by sword or fire, this night.
> If thou demand what cause of hate he has,
> Know that the villain wooes thine only child,
> Fair Rymenhild, and hopes to wear thy crown.
> E'en now he tarries in the maiden's bower,
> As he has often done, and talks with her
> With guileful tongue, and cunning show of love.
> Unless thou banish him thou art not safe
> In life or honour, for he knows no law."'

The king at first refused to believe the envious knight's report, but, going to Rymenhild's bower, he found apparent confirmation, for Horn was comforting the princess, and promising to wed her when he should have done worthy feats of arms. The king's wrath knew no bounds, and with words of harsh reproach he banished Horn at once, on pain of death. The young knight armed himself quickly and returned to bid farewell to his betrothed.

Horn's Banishment

'Dear heart,' said he, 'now thy dream has come true, and thy fish must needs break the net and be gone. The enemy whom I foreboded has wrought us woe. Farewell, mine own dear Rymenhild; I may no longer stay, but must wander in alien lands. If I do not return at the end of seven years take thyself a husband and tarry no longer for me. And now take me in your arms and kiss me, dear love, ere I go!' So they kissed each other and bade farewell, and Horn called to him his comrade Athulf, saying, 'True and faithful friend, guard well my dear love. Thou hast never forsaken me; now do thou keep Rymenhild for me. Then he rode away, and, reaching the haven, hired a good ship and sailed for Ireland, where he took service with King

Thurston, under the name of Cuthbert. In Ireland he became sworn brother to the king's two sons, Harold and Berild, for they loved him from the first moment they saw him, and were in no way jealous of his beauty and valour.

Horn Slays the Giant Emir

When Christmas came, and King Thurston sat at the banquet with all his lords, at noontide a giant strode into the hall, bearing a message of defiance. He came from the Saracens and challenged any three Irish knights to fight one Saracen champion. If the Irish won the pagans would withdraw from Ireland; if the Irish chiefs were slain the Saracens would hold the land. The combat was to be decided the next day at dawn. King Thurston accepted the challenge, and named Harold, Berild, and Cuthbert (as Horn was called) as the Christian champions, because they were the best warriors in Ireland; but Horn begged permission to speak, and said: 'Sir King, it is not right that one man should fight against three, and one heathen hound think to resist three Christian warriors. I will fight and conquer him alone, for I could as easily slay three of them.' At last the king allowed Horn to attempt the combat alone, and spent the night in sorrowful musing on the result of the contest, while Horn slept well and arose and armed himself cheerily. He then aroused the king, and the Irish troop rode out to a fair and level green lawn, where they found the emir with many companions awaiting them. The combat began at once, and Horn gave blows so mighty that the pagan onlookers fell swooning through very fear, till Horn said: 'Now, knights, rest for a time if it pleases you,' Then the Saracens spoke together, saying aloud that no man had ever so daunted them before except King Murry of Suddene.

This mention of his dead father aroused Horn, who now realized that he saw before him his father's murderers. His anger was kindled, he looked at his ring and thought of Rymenhild, and then, drawing his sword again, he rushed at the heathen champion. The giant fell pierced through the heart, and his companions fled to their ships, hotly pursued by Horn and his company. Much fighting there was, and in the hot strife near the ships the king's two sons, Harold and Berild, were both slain.

Horn Refuses the Throne

Sadly they were laid on a bier and brought back to the palace, their sorrowful father lamenting their early death; and when he had wept his fill the mournful king came into the hall where all his knights silently awaited him. Slowly he came up to Horn as he sat a little apart from the rest, and said: 'Cuthbert, wilt thou fulfil my desire? My heirs are slain, and thou art the best knight in Ireland for strength and beauty and valour; I implore thee to wed Reynild, my only daughter (now, alas! my only child), and to rule my realm. Wilt thou do so, and lift the burden of my cares from my weary shoulders?' But Horn replied: 'O Sir King, it were wrong for me to receive thy fair daughter and heir and rule thy realm, as thou dost offer. I shall do thee yet better service, my liege, before I die; and I know that thy grief will change ere seven years have passed away. When that time is over, Sir King, give me my reward: thou shalt not refuse me thy daughter when I desire her.' To this King Thurston agreed, and Horn dwelt in Ireland for seven years, and sent no word or token to Rymenhild all the time.

Rymenhild's Distress

In the meantime Princess Rymenhild was in great perplexity and trouble, for a powerful ruler, King Modi of Reynes, wooed her for his wife, and her own betrothed sent her no token of his life or love. Her father accepted the new suitor for her hand, and the day of the wedding was fixed, so that Rymenhild could no longer delay her marriage. In her extremity she besought Athulf to write letters to Horn, begging him to return and claim his bride and protect her; and these letters she delivered to several messengers, bidding them search in all lands until they found Sir Horn and gave the letters into his own hand. Horn knew nought of this, till one day in the forest he met a weary youth, all but exhausted, who told how he had sought Horn in vain. When Horn declared himself, the youth broke out into loud lamentations over Rymenhild's unhappy fate, and delivered the letter which explained all her distress. Now it was Horn's turn to weep bitterly for his love's troubles, and he bade the messenger return to his mistress and tell her to cease her tears, for Horn would be there in time to rescue her from her hated bridegroom. The youth returned joyfully, but as his boat neared the shore of Westernesse a storm arose and the messenger was drowned; so that Rymenhild, opening her tower door to look for expected succour, found her messenger lying dead at the foot of the tower, and felt that all hope was gone. She wept and wrung her hands, but nothing that she could do would avert the evil day.

Horn and King Thurston

As soon as Horn had read Rymenhild's letter he went to King Thurston and revealed the whole matter to him. He told of his own royal parentage, his exile, his knighthood, his betrothal to the princess, and his banishment; then of the death of the Saracen leader who had slain King Murry, and the vengeance he had taken. Then he ended:

> '"King Thurston, be thou wise, and grant my boon;
> Repay the service I have yielded thee;
> Help me to save my princess from this woe.
> I will take counsel for fair Reynild's fate,
> For she shall wed Sir Athulf, my best friend,
> My truest comrade and my doughtiest knight.
> If ever I have risked my life for thee
> And proved myself in battle, grant my prayer."'

To this the king replied: 'Childe Horn, do what thou wilt.'

Horn Returns on the Wedding-day

Horn at once invited Irish Knights to accompany him to Westernesse to rescue his love from a hateful marriage, and many cam eagerly to fight in the cause of the valiant Cuthbert who had defended Ireland for seven years. Thus it was with a goodly company that Horn took ship, and landed in King Ailmar's realm; and he came in a happy hour, for it was the wedding-day of Princess Rymenhild and King Modi of Reynes. The Irish knights landed and encamped in a wood, while Horn went on alone to learn tidings. Meeting a palmer, he asked the news, and the palmer replied: 'I have been at the wedding of Princess Rymenhild, and a sad sight it was, for the bride was wedded against her will, vowing she had a husband though he is a banished man. She would take no ring nor utter any vows; but the service was read, and afterwards King Modi took her to a strong castle, where not even a palmer was given entrance. I came away, for I could not endure the pity of it. The bride sits weeping sorely, and if report be true her heart is like to break with grief.'

Horn Is Disguised as a Palmer

'Come, palmer,' said Horn, 'lend me your cloak and scrip. I must see this strange bridal, and it may be I shall make some there repent of the wrong they have done to a helpless maiden. I will essay to enter.' The change was soon made, and Horn darkened his face and hands as if bronzed with Eastern suns, bowed his back, and gave his voice an old man's feebleness, so that no man would have known him; which done, he made his way to King Modi's new castle. Here he begged admittance for charity's sake, that he might share the broken bits of the wedding feast; but he was churlishly refused by the porter, who would not be moved by any entreaties. At last Horn lost all patience, and broke open the door, and threw the porter out over the drawbridge into the moat; then, once more assuming his disguise, he made his way into the hall and sat down in the beggars' row.

The Recognition

Rymenhild was weeping still, and her stern husband seemed only angered by her tears. Horn looked about cautiously, but saw no sign of Athulf, his trusted comrade; for he was at this time eagerly looking for his friend's coming from the lofty watch-tower, and lamenting that he could guard the princess no longer. At last, when the banquet was nearly over, Rymenhild rose to pour out wine for the guests, as the custom was then; and she bore a horn of ale or wine along the benches to each person there. Horn, sitting humbly on the ground, called out: 'Come, courteous Queen, turn to me, for we beggars are thirsty folk.' Rymenhild smiled sadly, and, setting down the horn, filled a bowl with brown ale, for she thought him a drunkard. 'Here, drink this, and more besides, if thou wilt; I never saw so bold a beggar,' she said. But Horn refused. He handed the bowl to the other beggars, and said: 'Lady, I will drink nought but from a silver cup, for I am not what you think me. I am no beggar, but a fisher, come from afar to fish at thy wedding feast. My net lies near by, and has lain there for seven years, and I am come to see if it has caught any fish. Drink to me, and drink to Horn from thy horn, for far have I journeyed.'

When the palmer spoke of fishing, and his seven-year-old net, Rymenhild felt cold at heart; she did not recognize him, but wondered greatly when he bade her drink 'to Horn.' She filled her cup and gave it to the palmer, saying, 'Drink thy fill, and then tell me if thou hast ever seen Horn in thy wanderings.' As the palmer drank, he dropped his ring into the cup; then he returned it to Rymenhild, saying, 'Queen, seek out what is in thy draught.' She said nothing then, but left the hall with her maidens and went to her bower, where she found the well-remembered ring she had given to Horn in token of betrothal. Greatly she feared that Horn was dead, and sent for the palmer, whom she questioned as to whence he had got the ring.

Horn's Stratagem

Horn thought he would test her love for him, since she had not recognized him, so he replied: 'By St Giles, lady, I have wandered many a mile, far into realms of the West, and there I found Sir Horn ready prepared to sail home to your land. He told me that he planned to reach the realm of Westernesse in time to see you before seven years had passed, and I embarked with him. The winds were favourable and we had a quick voyage, but, alas! he fell ill and died. When he lay dying he begged me piteously, "Take this ring from which I have never been parted, to my dear lady Rymenhild," and he kissed it many times and pressed it to his breast. May God give his soul rest in Paradise!'

When Rymenhild heard those terrible tidings she sighed deeply and said: 'O heart, burst now, for thou shalt never more have Horn, for love of whom thou hast been tormented so sorely!' Then she fell upon her bed and grasped the dagger which she had concealed there; for if Horn did not come in time she had planned to slay both her hateful lord and herself that very night. Now, in her misery, she set the dagger to her heart, and would have slain herself at once, had not the palmer interrupted her. Rushing forward, he exclaimed: 'Dear Queen and lady, I am Horn, thine own true love. Dost thou not recognize me? I am Childe Horn of Westernesse. Take me in thy arms, dear love and kiss me welcome home.' As Rymenhild stared incredulously at him, letting the dagger fall from her trembling hand, he hurriedly cast away his disguise, brushed off the disfiguring stain he had put on his cheeks, and stood up straight and strong, her own noble knight and lover. What joy they had together! How they told each other of all their adventures and troubles, and how they embraced and kissed each other!

Horn Slays King Modi

When their joy had become calmer, Horn said to his lady: 'Dear Rymenhild, I must leave thee now, and return to my knights, who are encamped in the forest. Within an hour I will return to the feast and give the king and his guests a stern lesson.' Then he flung away the palmer's cloak, and went forth in knightly array; while the princess went up to the watch-tower, where Athulf still scanned the sea for some sign of Horn's coming. Rymenhild said: 'Sir Athulf, true friend, go quickly to Horn, for he has arrived, and with him he brings a great army.' The knight gladly hastened to the courtyard, mounted his steed, and soon overtook Horn. They were greatly rejoiced to meet again, and had much to tell each other and to plan for that day's work.

In the evening Horn and his army reached the castle, where they found the gates undone for them by their friends within, and in a short but desperate conflict King Modi and all the guests at the banquet were slain, except Rymenhild, her father, and Horn's twelve comrades. Then a new wedding was celebrated, for King Ailmar durst not refuse his daughter to the victor, and the bridal was now one of real rejoicing, though the king was somewhat bitter of mood.

Horn's Daughter

When the hours wore on to midnight, Horn, sitting beside his bride, called for silence in the hall, and addressed the king thus: 'Sir King, I pray thee listen to my tale, for I have much to say and much to explain. My name is in sooth Horn, and I am the son of King Murry of Suddene, who was slain by the Saracens. Thou didst cherish me and give me knighthood, and I proved myself a true knight on the very day when I was dubbed. Thou didst love me then, but evil men accused me to thee and I was banished. For seven years I have lived in a strange land; but now that I have returned, I have won thy fair daughter as my bride. But I cannot dwell here in idleness while the heathen hold my father's land. I vow by the Holy Rood that I will not rest, and will not claim my wife, until I have purified Suddene from the infidel invaders, and can lay its crown at Rymenhild's feet. Do thou, O King, guard well my wife till my return.'

The king consented to this proposal, and, in spite of Rymenhild's grief, Horn immediately bade her farewell, and with his whole army embarked for Suddene, this time accompanied by Athulf, but leaving the rest of his comrades for the protection of his wife.

The Apostate Knight

The wind blew fair for Suddene, and the fleet reached the port. The warriors disembarked, and marched inland, to encamp for the night in a wood, where they could be hidden. Horn and Athulf set out at midnight to endeavour to obtain news of the foe, and soon found a solitary knight sleeping. They awoke him roughly, saying, 'Knight, awake! Why sleepest thou here? What dost thou guard?' The knight sprang lightly from the ground, saw their faces and the shining crosses on their shields, and cast down his eyes in shame, saying, 'Alas! I have served these pagans against my will. In time gone by I was a Christian, but now I am a coward renegade, who forsook his God for fear of death at the hands of the Saracens! I hate my infidel masters, but I fear them too, and they have forced me to guard this district and keep watch against Horn's return. If he should come to his own again how glad I should be! These infidels slew his father, and drove him into exile, with his twelve comrades, among whom was my own son, Athulf, who loved the prince as his own life. If the prince is yet alive, and my son also, God grant that I may see them both again! Then would I joyfully die.'

The Recognition

Horn answered quickly: 'Sir Knight, be glad and rejoice, for here are we, Horn and Athulf, come to avenge my father and retake my realm from the heathen.' Athulf's father was overcome with joy and shame; he hardly dared to embrace his son, yet the bliss of meeting was so great that he clasped Athulf in his arms and prayed his forgiveness for the disgrace he had brought upon him. The two young knights said nothing of his past weakness, but told him all their own adventures, and at last he said: 'What is your true errand hither? Can you two alone slay the heathen? Dear Childe Horn, what joy this will be to thy mother Godhild, who still lives in a solitary retreat, praying for thee and for the land!' Horn broke in on his speech with 'Blessed be the hour when I returned! Thank God that my mother yet lives! We are not alone, but I have an army of valiant Irish warriors, who will help me to regain my realm.'

The Reconquest of Suddene

Now the king blew his horn, and his host marched out from the wood and prepared to attack the Saracens. The news soon spread that Childe Horn had returned, and many men who had accepted the faith of Mahomet for fear of death now threw off the hated religion, joined the true king's army, and were rebaptized. The war was not long, for the Saracens had made themselves universally hated, and the inhabitants rose against them; so that in a short time the country was purged of the infidels, who were slain or fled to other lands. Then Horn brought his mother from her retreat, and together they purified the churches which had been desecrated, and restored the true faith. When the land of Suddene was again a Christian realm King Horn was crowned with solemn rites, and a great coronation feast was held, which lasted too long for Horn's true happiness.

Fikenhild Imprisons Rymenhild

During Horn's absence from Westernesse, his comrades watched carefully over Rymenhild; but her father, who was growing old, had fallen much under the influence of the plausible Fikenhild. From the day when Fikenhild had falsely accused Horn to the king, Ailmar had held him in honour as a loyal servant, and now he had such power over the old ruler that when he demanded Rymenhild's hand in marriage, saying that Horn was dead in Suddene, the king dared not refuse, and the princess was bidden to make ready for a new bridal. For this day Fikenhild had long been prepared; he had built a massive fortress on a promontory, which at high tide was surrounded by the sea, but was easy of access at the ebb; thither he now led the weeping princess, and began a wedding feast which was to last all day, and to end only with the marriage ceremony at night.

Horn's Dream

That same night, before the feast, King Horn had a terrible dream. He thought he saw his wife taken on board ship; soon the ship began to sink, and Rymenhild held out her hands for rescue, but Fikenhild, standing in safety on shore, beat her back into the waves with his sword. With the agony of the sight Horn awoke, and, calling his comrade Athulf, said: 'Friend we must depart to-day. My wife is in danger from false Fikenhild, whom I have trusted too much. Let us delay no longer, but go at once. If God will, I hope to release her, and to punish Fikenhild. God grant we come in time!' With some few chosen knights, King Horn and Athulf set out, and the ship drove darkling through the sea, they knew not whither. All the night they drifted on, and in the morning found themselves beneath a newly built castle, which none of them had seen before.

Horn's Disguise

While they were seeking to moor their boat to the shore, one of the castle windows looking out to sea opened, and they saw a knight standing and gazing seaward, whom they speedily recognized; it was Athulf's cousin, Sir Arnoldin, one of the twelve comrades, who had accompanied the princess thither in the hope that he might yet save her from Fikenhild; he was now looking, as a forlorn hope, over the sea, though he believed Horn was dead. His joy was great when he saw the knights, and he came out to them and speedily told them of Rymenhild's distress and the position of affairs in the castle. King Horn was not at a loss for an expedient even in this distress. He quickly disguised himself and a few of his comrades as minstrels, harpers, fiddlers, and jugglers. Then, rowing to the mainland, he waited till low tide, and made his way over the beach to the castle, accompanied by his disguised comrades. Outside the castle walls they began to play and sing, and Rymenhild heard them, and, asking what the sounds were, gave orders that the minstrels should be admitted. They sat on benches low down the hall, tuning their harps and fiddles and watching the bride, who seemed unhappy and pale When Horn sang a lay of true love and happiness, Rymenhild swooned for grief, and the king was touched to the heart with bitter remorse that he had tried her constancy so long, and had allowed her to endure such hardships and misery for his sake.

Death of Fikenhild

King Horn now glanced down and saw the ring of betrothal on his finger, where he had worn it ever, except that fateful day when he had given it as a token of recognition to Rymenhild. He thought of his wife's sufferings, and his mind was made up. Springing from the minstrels' bench, he strode boldly up the hall, throwing off his disguise, and, shouting, 'I am King Horn! False Fikenhild, thou shalt die!' he slew the villain in the midst of his men. Horn's comrades likewise flung off their disguise, and soon overpowered the few of the household who cared to fight in their dead master's cause. The castle was taken for King Ailmar, who was persuaded to nominate Sir Arnoldin his heir, and the baronage of Westernesse did homage to him as the next king. Horn and his fair wife begged the good old steward Sir Athelbrus to go with them to Suddene, and on the way they touched at Ireland, where Reynild, the king's fair daughter, was induced to look favourably on Sir Athulf and accept him for her husband. The land of King Modi, which had now no ruler, was committed to the care of Sir Athelbrus, and Horn and Rymenhild at last reached Suddene, where the people received their fair queen with great joy, and where they dwelt in happiness till their lives' end.

Robin Hood

IN THE interwoven history of conquest and resistance which makes up the tapestry of early English history, Robin Hood is a Saxon champion battling against the overwhelming power of the Normans. Yet the identity of the famous Outlaw of Sherwood Forest has been a vexed question ever since he first sprang to fame in the ballads and songs of the twelfth century. No two authorities seem able to agree as to his origins, dates, or whether he was a historical personage or a wholly mythical figure. Historians, both amateur and professional, have for years been bringing out new books in which they claim to have found 'the real Robin Hood'.

More recent studies have sought to push the boundaries of the story further out into recorded time – seeking Robin Hood among the records of government and law enforcement, in the ballads of the twelfth to fourteenth centuries, and in the folk memory of the people of Britain. For them, Robin is either a product of the ballad-maker's muse, or a literary fabrication based on the lives and deeds of several outlaws, or on garbled memories of an actual person whose real life bore little or no resemblance to the romanticized songs of the ballad-makers.

The so-called 'mythological school' has, at the same time, poured scorn on these attempts, maintaining that Robin never existed as a real person at all, and that to seek him among the fragmentary records of the Middle Ages is a waste of time. These writers have made a case for Robin Hood as a figure of myth and folklore. However, in every case their conclusions lack the detailed study of folklore, tradition, and myth necessary to their credibility. They have thus, in their turn, been dismissed.

Neither side seems to have seriously considered that they might both be right, that a historical personage or personages might have inherited the qualities and archetypal demeanours of an older figure or figures, known originally from ancient myth and later from literary history and folklore belief. Foremost among such ancient characters is the Green Man, a personification of the power of the natural world, who has continued to haunt the minds and imaginations of people in many different parts of the world ever since.

The very fact that the presence of Robin – and through him of the Green Man – has come down to us at all is due to a number of complex reasons, one of the foremost being the continuing popularity of the Robin Hood myths in modern dress through film, television and novelization. Both Robin and the Green Man have fed each other, and it is at the centre of this interaction that the most powerful elements of the living greenwood myth have their place.

It is this mythic tradition which informs the ballads and plays, the songs and dances of Robin Hood. It enlivened the dark days of winter for our medieval ancestors, and it helped them welcome back the spring. Robin and Marian represent a freedom since lost to us, the freedom to escape to the woods and live at peace there. They remind us of the times when, in our childhood, we made bows and arrows out of pieces of stick and played at Robin Hood and the Sheriff of Nottingham.

The mystery which lies at the heart of the greenwood is a green mystery; when the greenness is brought inside – as in the Green Men found carved on medieval church roof bosses – it is spent, it dies. In the tales of Robin Hood it is set free, and with it all who seek to experience the joyous celebrations of May Day, when Robin and Marian come together and are crowned with the blossom which signifies both their union and the birth of the new season.

This may all seem a far cry from the idea of the 'Jolly Outlaw of Sherwood' so beloved of nineteenth- and early-twentieth-century children's writers. Yet the fact that Robin is a far older figure is reflected in the ballads and tales which circulated about him from the twelfth century onwards. The version recorded here is taken from the earliest complete story of which we know, 'The Gest of Robin Hood', which was not printed until 1508 but is clearly based on much earlier ballads previously circulating orally. It reflects a later view of the outlaw, and sites his field of activity in the Forest of Barnsdale in Yorkshire rather than in Sherwood. The characters of Little John, Will Scarlet and Much the miller's son are already in place, though there is, as yet, no Maid Marian or Friar Tuck. The piece reflects the time when it was written presenting us with a harsh view of life in the forest and representing the Church as a greedy, avaricious organization concerned more with fiscal profits than with souls. Robin, of course, stands for the downtrodden peasant, and for the inalienable rights of the individual although, interestingly, in this story he is shown helping a poor knight who has fallen foul of a greedy abbot. His undoubted chivalry and courteous treatment of friend and foe alike, mark him out as a worthy candidate for inclusion here.

 Of the many ballads of Robin Hood which exist, I have chosen the following to give a flavour of the original:

In Sherwood lived stout Robin Hood,
  An archer great, none greater;
His bow and shafts were sure and good,
  Yet Cupid's were much better.
Robin could shoot at many a hart and miss,
  Cupid at first could hit a hart of his.
    Hey jolly Robin, ho jolly Robin,
      Hey jolly Robin Hood,
    Love finds out me, as well as thee,
      To follow me,
    To follow me to the green wood.

A noble thief was Robin Hood,
  Wise was he could deceive him,
Yet Marian, in his bravest mood,
  Could of his heart bereave him.
No greater thief lies hidden under skies
  Than beauty closely lodged in women's eyes.
    Hey jolly Robin, etc.

Robin Hood Seeks a Guest

At one time Robin Hood lived in the noble forest of Barnesdale, in Yorkshire. He had but few of his merry men with him, for his headquarters were in the glorious forest of Sherwood. Just now, however, the Sheriff of Nottinghamshire was less active in his endeavours to put down the band of outlaws, and the leader had wandered farther north than usual. Robin's companions were his three dearest comrades and most loyal followers, Little John (so called because of his great stature), Will Scarlet, Robin's cousin, and Much, the miller's son. These three were all devoted to their leader, and never left his side, except at such times as he sent them away on his business.

On this day Robin was leaning against a tree, lost in thought, and his three followers grew impatient; they knew that before dinner could be served there were the three customary Masses to hear, and their leader gave no sign of being ready for Mass. Robin always heard three Masses before his dinner, one of the Father, one of the Holy Spirit, and the last of Our Lady, who was his patron saint and protector. As the three yeomen were growing hungry, Little John ventured to address him. 'Master, it would do you good if you would dine early to-day, for you have fasted long.' Robin aroused himself and smiled. 'Ah, Little John, methinks care for thine own appetite hath a share in that speech, as well as care for me. But in sooth I care not to dine alone. I would have a stranger guest, some abbot or bishop or baron, who would pay us for our hospitality. I will not dine till a guest be found, and I leave it to you three to find him.' Robin turned away, laughing at the crestfallen faces of his followers, who had not counted on such a vague commission; but Little John, quickly recovering himself, called to him: 'Master, tell us, before we leave you, where we shall meet, and what sort of people we are to capture and bring to you in the greenwood.'

The Outlaws' Rules

'You know that already,' said their master. 'You are to do no harm to women, nor to any company in which a woman is travelling; this is in honour of our dear Lady. You are to be kind and gentle to husbandmen and toilers of all degrees, to worthy knights and yeomen, to gallant squires, and to all children and helpless people; but sheriffs (especially him of Nottingham), bishops, and prelates of all kinds, and usurers in Church and State, you may regard as your enemies, and may rob, beat, and despoil in any way. Meet me with your guest at our great trysting oak in the forest, and be speedy, for dinner must wait until the visitor has arrived.' 'Now may God send us a suitable traveller soon,' said Little John, 'for I am hungry for dinner now.' 'So am I,' said each of the others, and Robin laughed again. 'Go ye all three, with bows and arrows in hand, and I will stay alone at the trysting tree and await your coming. As no man passes this way, you can walk up to the willow plantation and take your stand on Watling Street; there you will soon meet with likely travellers, and I will accept the first who appears. I will find means to have dinner ready against your return, and we will hope that our visitor's generosity will compensate us for the trouble of cooking his dinner.'

'Little John caught the horse by the bridle'

Robin Hood's Guest

The three yeomen, taking their longbows in hand and arrows in their belts, walked up through the willow plantation to a place on Watling Street where another road crossed it; but there was no one in sight. As they stood with bows in hand, looking towards the forest of Barnesdale, they saw in the distance a knight riding in their direction. As he drew nearer they were struck by his appearance, for he rode as a man who had lost all interest in life; his clothes were disordered, he looked neither to right nor left, but drooped his head sadly, while one foot hung in the stirrup and the other dangled slackly in the air. The yeomen had never seen so doleful a rider; but, sad as he was, this was a visitor and must be taken to Robin; accordingly Little John stepped forward and caught the horse by the bridle.

Little John Escorts the Knight

The knight raised his head and looked blankly at the outlaw, who at once doffed his cap, saying, 'Welcome, Sir Knight! I give you, on my master's behalf, a hearty welcome to the greenwood. Gentle knight, come now to my master who hath waited three hours, fasting, for your approach before he would dine. Dinner is prepared, and only tarries your courteous appearance.' The stranger knight seemed to consider this address carefully, for he sighed.deeply, and then said: 'I cry thee mercy, good fellow, for the delay, though I wot not how I am the cause thereof. But who is thy master?' Little John replied: 'My master's name is Robin Hood, and I am sent to guide you to him.' The knight said: 'So Robin Hood is thy leader? I have heard of him, and know him to be a good yeoman; therefore I am ready to accompany thee, though, in good sooth, I had intended to eat my midday meal at Blythe or Doncaster to-day. But it matters little where a broken man dines!'

Robin Hood's Feast

The three yeomen conducted the knight along the forest ways to the trysting oak where Robin awaited them. As they went they observed that the knight was weeping silently for some great distress, but their courtesy forbade them to make any show of noticing his grief. When the appointed spot was reached, Robin stepped forward and courteously greeted his guest, with head uncovered and bended knee, and welcomed him gladly to the wild greenwood. 'Welcome, Sir Knight, to our greenwood feast! I have waited three hours for a guest, and now Our Lady has sent you to me we can dine, after we have heard Mass.' The knight said nothing but, 'God save you, good Robin, and all your merry men'; and then very devoutly they heard the three Masses, sung by Friar Tuck. By this time others of the outlaw band had appeared, having returned from various errands, and a gay company sat down to a banquet as good as any the knight had ever eaten.

Robin Converses with the Knight

There was abundance of good things – venison and game of all kinds, swans and river-fowl and fish, with bread and good wine. Every one seemed joyous, and merry jests went round that jovial company, till even the careworn guest began to smile, and then to laugh outright. At this Robin was well pleased, for he saw that his visitor was a good man, and was glad to have lifted the burden of his care, even if only for a few minutes; so he smiled cheerfully at the knight and said: 'Be merry, Sir Knight, I pray, and eat heartily of our food, for it is with great goodwill that we offer it to you.' 'Thanks, good Robin,' replied the knight. 'I have enjoyed my dinner to-day greatly; for three weeks I have not had so good a meal. If I ever pass by this way again I will do my best to repay you in kind; as good a dinner will I try to provide as you have given me.'

Robin Demands Payment

The outlaw chief seemed to be affronted by this suggestion, and replied, with a touch of pride in his manner: 'Thanks for your proffer, Sir Knight, but, by Heaven! no man has ever yet deemed me a glutton. While I eat one dinner I am not accustomed to look eagerly for another – one is enough for me. But as for you, my guest, I think it only fitting that you should pay before you go; a yeoman was never meant to pay for a knight's banquet.' The knight blushed, and looked confused for a moment, and then said: 'True, Robin, and gladly would I reward you for my entertainment, but I have no money worth offering; even all I have would not be worthy of your acceptance, and I should be shamed in your eyes, and those of your men.'

The Knight's Poverty

'Is that the truth?' asked Robin, making a sign to Little John, who arose, and, going to the knight's steed, unstrapped a small coffer, which he brought back and placed before his master. 'Search it, Little John,' said he, and 'You sir, tell me the very truth, by your honour as a belted knight.' 'It is truth, on my honour, that I have but ten shillings,' replied the knight, 'and if Little John searches he will find no more.' 'Open the coffer,' said Robin, and Little John took it away to the other side of the trysting oak, where he emptied its contents on his outspread cloak, and found exactly ten shillings. Returning to his master, who sat at his ease, drinking and gaily conversing with his anxious guest, Little John whispered: 'The knight has told the truth,' and thereupon Robin exclaimed aloud: 'Sir Knight, I will not take one penny from you; you may rather borrow of me if you have need of more money, for ten shillings is but a miserable sum for a knight. But tell me now, if it be your pleasure, how you come to be in such distress.' As he looked inquiringly at the stranger, whose blush had faded once, only to be renewed as he found his word of honour doubted, he noticed how thin and threadbare were his clothes and how worn his russet leather shoes; and he was grieved to see so noble-seeming a man in such a plight.

The Knight's Story

Yet Robin meant to fathom the cause of the knight's trouble, for then, perhaps, he would be able to help him, so he continued pitilessly: 'Tell me just one word, which I will keep secret from all other men: were you driven by compulsion to take up knighthood, or urged to beg it by reason of the ownership of some small estate; or have you wasted your old inheritance with fines for brawling and strife, or in gambling and riotousness, or in borrowing at usury? All of these are fatal to a good estate.'

The knight replied: 'Alas! good Robin, none of these hath been my undoing. My ancestors have all been knights for over a hundred years, and I have not lived wastefully, but soberly and sparely. As short a time ago as last year I had over four hundred pounds saved, which I could spend freely among my neighbours, and my income was four hundred pounds a year, from my land; but now my only possessions are my wife and children. This is the work of God's hand, and to Him I commit me to amend my estate in His own good time.'

How the Money Was Lost

'But how have you so soon lost this great wealth?' asked Robin incredulously; and the knight replied sadly: 'Ah, Robin, you have no son, or you would know that a father will give up all to save his first-born. I have one gallant son, and when I went on the Crusade with our noble Prince Edward I left him at home to guard my lands, for he was twenty years old, and was a brave and comely youth. When I returned, after two years' absence, it was to find him in great danger, for in a public tournament he had slain in open fight a knight of Lancashire and a bold young squire. He would have died a shameful death had I not spent all my ready money and other property to save him from prison, for his enemies were mighty and unjust; and even that was not enough, for I was forced to mortgage my estates for more money. All my land lies in pledge to the abbot of St Mary's Abbey, in York, and I have no hope to redeem it. I was riding to York when your men found me.'

The Sum Required

'For what sum is your land pledged?' asked the master-outlaw; and the knight replied: 'The Abbot lent me four hundred pounds, though the value of the land is far beyond that.' 'What will you do if you fail to redeem your land?' asked Robin. 'I shall leave England at once, and journey once more to Jerusalem, and tread again the sacred Hill of Calvary, and never more return to my native land. That will be my fate, for I see no likelihood of repaying the loan, and I will not stay to see strangers holding my father's land. Farewell, my friend Robin, farewell to you all! Keep the ten shillings; I would have paid more if I could, but that is the best I can give you.' 'Have you no friends at home?' asked Robin; and the knight said: 'Many friends I thought I had, sir. They were very kind and helpful in my days of prosperity, when I did not need them; now they will not know me, so much has my poverty seemed to alter my face and appearance.

Robin Offers a Loan

This pitiful story touched the hearts of the simple and kindly outlaws; they wept for pity, and cared not to hide their tears from each other, until Robin made them all pledge their guest in bumpers of good red wine. Then their chief asked, as if continuing his own train of thought: 'Have you any friends who will act as sureties for the repayment of the loan?' 'None at all,' replied the knight hopelessly, 'but God Himself, who suffered on the Tree for us.' This last reply angered Robin, who thought it savoured too much of companionship with the fat and hypocritical monks whom he hated, and he retorted sharply: 'No such tricks for me! Do you think I will take such a surety, or even one of the saints, in return for good solid gold? Get some more substantial surety, or no gold shall you have from me. I cannot afford to waste my money.'

The Knight Offers Surety

The knight replied, sighing heavily: 'If you will not take these I have no earthly surety to offer; and in Heaven there is only our dear Lady. I have served her truly, and she has never failed me till now, when her servant, the abbot, is playing me so cruel a trick.' 'Do you give Our Lady as your surety?' said Robin Hood. 'I would take her bond for any sum, for throughout all England you could find no better surety than our dear Lady, who has always been gracious to me. She is enough security. Go, Little John, to my treasury and bring me four hundred pounds, well counted, with no false or clipped coin therein.'

Robin Hood's Gifts

Little John, accompanied by Much, the careful treasurer of the band, went quickly to the secret place where the master-outlaw kept his gold. Very carefully they counted out the coins, testing each, to see that it was of full weight and value. Then, on the suggestion of Little John, they provided the knight with new clothing, even to boots and spurs, and finally supplied him with two splendid horses, one for riding and one to carry his baggage and the coffer of gold.

The guest watched all these preparations with bewildered eyes, and turned to Robin, crying, 'Why have you done all this for me, a perfect stranger?' 'You are no stranger, but Our Lady's messenger. She sent you to me, and Heaven grant you may prove true.'

The Bond of Repayment

'God grant it,' echoed the knight. 'But, Robin, when shall I repay this loan, and where? Set me a day, and I will keep it.' 'Here,' replied the outlaw, 'under this greenwood tree, and in a twelvemonth's time; so will you have time to regain your friends and gather your rents from your redeemed lands. Now farewell, Sir Knight; and since it is not meet for a worthy knight to journey unattended, I will lend you also my comrade, Little John, to be your squire, and to do you yeoman service, if need be.' The knight bade farewell to Robin and his generous followers, and was turning to ride away, when he suddenly stopped and addressed the master-outlaw: 'In faith, good Robin, I had forgotten one thing. You know not my name. I am Sir Richard of the Lea, and my land lies in Uterysdale.' 'As for that,' said Robin

Hood, 'I trouble not myself. Your are Our Lady's messenger; that is enough for me.' So Sir Richard rode gladly away, blessing the generous outlaw who lent him money to redeem his land, and a stout yeoman to defend the loan.

Sir Richard's Journey

As the knight and his new servant rode on, Sir Richard called to his man, saying, 'I must by all means be in York to-morrow, to pay the abbot of St Mary's four hundred pounds; if I fail of my day I shall lose my land and lordship for ever'; and Little John answered: 'Fear not, master; we will surely be there in time enough.' Then they rode on, and reached York early on the last day of the appointed time.

The Abbot and Prior of St Mary

In the meantime the abbot of St Mary's was counting that Sir Richard's lands were safely his; he had no pity for the poor unlucky knight, but rather exulted in the legal cruelty which he could inflict. Very joyfully he called aloud, early that morn: 'A twelvemonth ago to-day we lent four hundred pounds to a needy knight, Sir Richard of the Lea, and unless he comes by noon to-day to repay the money he will lose all his land and be disinherited, and our abbey will be the richer by a fat estate, worth four hundred pounds a year. Our Lady grant that he keep not his day.' 'Shame on you!' cried the prior. 'This poor knight may be ill, or beyond the sea; he may be in hunger and cold as well as poverty, and it will be a foul wrong if you declare his land forfeit.'

'This is the set day,' replied the abbot, 'and he is not here.' 'You dare not escheat his estates yet,' replied the prior stubbornly. 'It is too early in the day; until noon the lands are still Sir Richard's, and no man shall take them ere the clock strikes. Shame on your conscience and your greed, to do a good knight such foul wrong! I would willingly pay a hundred pounds myself to prevent it.'

'Beshrew your meddlesome temper!' cried the abbot. 'You are always crossing me! But I have with me the Lord Chief Justice, and he will declare my legal right.' Just at that moment the high cellarer of the abbey entered to congratulate the abbot on Sir Richard's absence. 'He is dead or ill, and we shall have the spending of four hundred pounds a year,' quoth he.

Sir Richard Returns

On his arrival Sir Richard had quietly gone round to his old tenants in York, and had a goodly company of them ready to ride with him, but he was minded to test the charity and true religion of the abbot, and bade his followers assume pilgrims' robes. Thus attired, the company rode to the abbey gate, where the porter recognized Sir Richard, and the news of his coming, carried to the abbot and justice, caused them great grief; but the prior rejoiced, hoping that a cruel injustice would be prevented. As they dismounted the porter loudly called grooms to lead the horses into the stable and have them relieved of their burdens, but Sir Richard would not allow it, and left Little John to watch over them at the abbey portal.

The Abbot and Sir Richard

Then Sir Richard came humbly into the hall, where a great banquet was in progress, and knelt down in courteous salutation to the abbot and his guests; but the prelate, who had made up his mind what conduct to adopt, greeted him coldly, and many men did not return his salutation at all. Sir Richard spoke aloud: 'Rejoice, Sir Abbot, for I am come to keep my day.' 'That is well,' replied the monk, 'but hast thou brought the money?' 'No money have I, not one penny,' continued Sir Richard sadly. 'Pledge me in good red wine, Sir Justice,' cried the abbot callously; 'the land is mine. And what dost thou here, Sir Richard, a broken man, with no money to pay thy debt?' 'I am come to beg you to grant me a longer time for repayment.' 'Not one minute past the appointed hour,' said the exultant prelate. 'Thou hast broken pledge, and thy land is forfeit.'

Sir Richard Implores the Justice

Still kneeling, Sir Richard turned to the justice and said: 'Good Sir Justice, be my friend and plead for me.' 'No,' he replied, 'I hold to the law, and can give thee no help.' 'Gentle abbot, have pity on me, and let me have my land again, and I will be the humble servant of your monastery till I have repaid in full your four hundred pounds.' Then the cruel prelate swore a terrible oath that never should the knight have his land again, and no one in the hall would speak for him, kneeling there poor, friendless, and alone; so at last he began to threaten violence. 'Unless I have my land again,' quoth he, 'some of you here shall dearly abide it. Now may I see the poor man has no friends, for none will stand by me in my need.'

The Justice Suggests a Compromise

The hint of violence made the abbot furiously angry, and, secure in his position and the support of the justice, he shouted loudly: 'Out, thou false knight! Out of my hall!' Then at last Sir Richard rose to his feet in just wrath. 'Thou liest, Sir Abbot; foully thou liest! I was never a false knight. In joust and tourney I have adventured as far and as boldly as any man alive. There is no true courtesy in thee, abbot, to suffer a knight to kneel so long.' The quarrel now seemed so serious that the justice intervened, saying to the angry prelate, 'What will you give me if I persuade him to sign a legal deed of release? Without it you will never hold this land in peace.' 'You shall have a hundred pounds for yourself,' said the abbot, and the justice nodded in token of assent.

Sir Richard Pays the Money

Now Sir Richard thought it was time to drop the mask, for noon was nigh, and he would not risk his land again. Accordingly he cried: 'Nay, but not so easily shall ye have my lands. Even if you were to pay a thousand pounds more you should not hold my father's estate. Have here your money back again'; and, calling for Little John, he bade him bring into the hall his coffer with the bags inside. Then he counted out on the table four hundred good golden pounds, and said sternly: 'Abbot, here is your money again. Had you but been courteous to me I would have rewarded you well; now take your money, give me a quittance, and I will take my lands once more. Ye are all witnesses that I have kept my day and have paid in full.' Thereupon Sir Richard strode haughtily out of the hall, and rode home gladly to his recovered lands in Uterysdale, where he and his family ever prayed for Robin Hood. The abbot of St Mary's was bitterly enraged, for he had lost the fair lands of Sir Richard of the Lea and had received a bare four hundred pounds again. As for Little John, he went back to the forest and told his master the whole story, to Robin Hood's great satisfaction, for he enjoyed the chance of thwarting the schemes of a wealthy and usurious prelate.

Sir Richard Sets Out to Repay the Loan

When a year had passed all but a few days, Sir Richard of the Lea said to his wife: 'Lady, I must shortly go to Barnesdale to repay Robin Hood the loan which saved my lands, and would fain take him some small gift in addition; what do you advise?' 'Sir Richard, I would take a hundred bows of Spanish yew and a hundred sheaves of arrows, peacock-feathered, or grey-goose-feathered; methinks that will be to Robin a most acceptable gift.'

Sir Richard followed his wife's advice, and on the morning of the appointed day set out to keep his tryst at the outlaws' oak in Barnesdale, with the money duly counted, and the bows and arrows for his present to the outlaw chief.

The Wrestling

As he rode, however, at the head of his troop he passed through a village where there was a wrestling contest, which he stayed to watch. He soon saw that the victorious wrestler, who was a stranger to the village, would be defrauded of his well-earned prize, which consisted of a white bull, a noble charger gaily caparisoned, a gold ring, a pipe of wine, and a pair of embroidered gloves. This seemed so wrong to Sir Richard that he stayed to defend the right, for love of Robin Hood and of justice, and kept the wrestling ring in awe with his well-appointed troop of men, so that the stranger was allowed to claim his prize and carry it off. Sir Richard, anxious not to arouse the hostility of the villagers, bought the pipe of wine from the winner, and, setting it abroach, allowed all who would to drink; and so, in a tumult of cheers and blessings, he rode away to keep his tryst. By this time, however, it was nearly three in the afternoon, and he should have been there at twelve. He comforted himself with the thought that Robin would forgive the delay, for the sake of its cause, and so rode on comfortably enough at the head of his gallant company.

Robin's Impatience

In the meantime Robin had waited patiently at the trysting tree till noon, but when the hour passed and Sir Richard had not appeared he began to grow impatient.

'Master, let us dine,' said Little John. 'I cannot; I fear Our Lady is angered with me, for she has not sent me my money,' returned the leader; but his follower replied: 'The money is not due till sunset, master, and Our Lady is true, and so is Sir Richard; have no fear.' 'Do you three walk up through the willow plantation to Watling Street, as you did last year, and bring me a guest,' said Robin Hood. 'He may be a messenger, a minstrel, a poor man, but he will come in God's name.

The Monks Approach

Again the three yeomen, Little John, Will Scarlet, and Much the miller's son, took bow in hand and set out for Watling Street; but this time they had not long to wait, for they at once saw a little procession approaching. Two black monks rode at the head; then followed seven sumpter-mules and a train of fifty-two men, so that the clerics rode in almost royal state. 'Seest thou yon monks?' said Little John. 'I will pledge my soul that they have brought our pay.' 'But they are fifty-four, and we are but three,' said Scarlet. 'Unless we bring them to dinner we dare not face our master,' cried Little John. 'Look well to your bows, your strings and arrows, and have stout hearts and steady hands. I will take the foremost monk, for life or death.'

The Capture of the Black Monk

The three outlaws stepped out into the road from the shelter of the wood; they bent their bows and held their arrows on the string, and Little John cried aloud: 'Stay, churlish monk, or thou goest to thy death, and it will be on thine own head! Evil on thee for keeping our master fasting so long.' 'Who is your master?' asked the bewildered monk; and Little John replied: 'Robin Hood.' The monk tossed his head. 'He is a foul thief,' cried he, 'and will come to a bad end. I have heard no good of him all my days.' So speaking, he tried to ride forward and trample down the three yeomen; but Little John cried: 'Thou liest, churlish monk, and thou shalt rue the lie. He is a good yeoman of this forest, and has bidden thee to dine with him this day'; and Much, drawing his bow, shot the monk to the heart, so that he fell to the ground dead. The other black monk was taken, but all his followers fled, except a little page, and a groom who tended the sumpter-mules; and thus, with Little John's help and guidance, the panic-stricken cleric and his train of baggage were brought to Robin under the trysting tree.

The Outlaw's Feast

Robin Hood doffed his cap and greeted his guest with all courtesy, but the monk would not reply, and Little John's account of their meeting made it evident that he was a churlish and unwilling guest. However, he was obliged to celebrate the three usual Masses, was given water for his ablutions before the banquet, and then when the whole fellowship was assembled he was set in the place of honour at the feast, and reverently served by Robin himself. 'Be of good cheer, Sir Monk,' said Robin. 'Where is your abbey when you are at home, and who is your patron saint?' 'I am of St Mary's Abbey, in York, and, simple though I be, I am the high cellarer.'

The High Cellarer and the Suretyship

'For Our Lady's sake,' said Robin, 'we will give this monk the best of cheer. Drink to me, Sir Monk; the wine is good. But I fear Our Lady is wroth with me, for she has not sent me my money.' 'Fear not, master,' returned Little John; 'this monk is her cellarer, and no doubt she has made him her messenger and he carries our money with him.' 'That is likely,' replied Robin. 'Sir Monk, Our Lady was surety for a little loan between a good knight and me, and to-day the money was to be repaid. If you have brought it, pay it to me now, and I will thank you heartily.' The monk was quite amazed, and cried aloud: 'I have never heard of such a suretyship'; and as he spoke he looked so anxiously at his sumpter-mules that Robin guessed there was gold in their pack-saddles.

The Monk is Searched

Accordingly the leader feigned sudden anger. 'Sir Monk, how dare you defame our dear Lady? She is always true and faithful, and as you say you are her servant, no doubt she has made you her messenger to bring my money. Tell me truly how much you have in your coffers, and I will thank you for coming so punctually.' The monk replied: 'Sir, I have only twenty marks in my bags'; to which Robin answered: 'If that be all, and you have told the truth, I will not touch one penny; rather will I lend you some if you need it; but if I find more, I will leave none, Sir Monk, for a religious man should have no silver to spend in luxury.' Now the monk looked very greatly alarmed, but he dared make no protest, as Little John began to search his bags and coffers.

Success of the Search

When Little John opened the first coffer he emptied its contents, as before, into his cloak, and counted eight hundred pounds, with which he went to Robin Hood, saying, 'Master, the monk has told the truth; here are twenty marks of his own, and eight hundred pounds which Our Lady has sent you in return for your loan.' When Robin heard that he cried to the miserable monk: 'Did I not say so, monk? Is not Our Lady the best surety a man could have? Has she not repaid me twice? Go back to your abbey and say that if ever St Mary's monks need a friend they shall find one in Robin Hood.'

The Monk Departs

'Where were you journeying?' asked the outlaw leader. 'To settle accounts with the bailiffs of our manors,' replied the cellarer; but he was in truth journeying to London, to obtain powers from the king against Sir Richard of the Lea. Robin thought for a moment, and then said: 'Ah, then we must search your other coffer,' and in spite of the cellarer's indignant protests he was deprived of all the money that second coffer contained. Then he was allowed to depart, vowing bitterly that a dinner in Blythe or Doncaster would have cost him much less dear.

Sir Richard Arrives

Late that afternoon Sir Richard of the Lea and his little company arrived at the trysting tree, and full courteously the knight greeted his deliverer and apologized for his delay. Robin asked of his welfare, and the knight told of his protection of the poor wrestler, for which Robin thanked him warmly. When he would fain have repaid the loan the generous outlaw refused to accept the money, though he took with hearty thanks the bows and arrows. In answer to the knight's inquiries, Robin said that he had been paid the money twice over before he came; and he told, to his debtor's great amusement, the story of the high cellarer and his eight hundred pounds, and concluded: 'Our Lady owed me no more than four hundred pounds, and she now gives you, by me, the other four hundred. Take them, with her blessing, and if ever you need more come to Robin Hood.'

So Sir Richard returned to Uterysdale, and long continued to use his power to protect the bold outlaws, and Robin Hood dwelt securely in the greenwood, doing good to the poor and worthy, but acting as a thorn in the sides of all oppressors and tyrants.

Hereward the Wake

THE subject of this final story is one of the most elusive of all our native heroes. Yet he is a pivotal figure in the tradition of heroic resistance to the successive waves of conquerors who overran this country.

He is first mentioned in a single sentence in *The Anglo-Saxon Chronicle* which refers to a band of disaffected farm tenants, Danes and English, who attacked the abbey of Peterborough, as 'Herward and his gang'. From this the legends grew and were finally gathered in the *De Gestis Herwardi Saxonis* (*The Life of Hereward the Saxon*) on which the present retelling is based.

Tradition says that Hereward was born at Bourne in Lincolnshire, and the *Domesday Book* confirms that he held lands in that county, as well as in Warwickshire and Worcestershire. Nothing certain is known of his parents, despite the tradition which says that he was the son of Earl Leofric and Lady Godiva (she of the famous ride). This would have made him an uncle to Edwin and Morcar, the last surviving members of the English royal house. However, this is probably a confusion arising from the fact that Hereward served an Abbot Leofric, who was the Earl's nephew.

Curiously, the story told here omits the real reason for Hereward's undying place in the history and hero myths of England – his spirited and, for a long while, successful defence of the Isle of Ely against the might of the Norman conquerors.

The story begins in 1069 when the Saxon Abbot of Peterborough died, to be replaced by a Norman named Turold, a soldier as well as a prelate, to whom was given the task of subduing the Saxon rabble around Peterborough. Hereward, at the head of the band of angry tenants referred to in the quotation from *The Anglo-Saxon Chronicle* below, outmanoeuvred the Normans and attacked the abbey, sacking it thoroughly. He then retired to the Isle of Ely, which was surrounded by a maze of fens and narrow rivers, making it virtually impregnable.

Hereward continued to hold the place against all attempts by the Normans to overwhelm him. Groups of English warriors and thegns marched to join him, making him the figurehead and Ely the last stronghold of Saxon resistance to the Normans.

On one occasion Duke William (now crowned King of England) was said to have employed the services of a witch, who led the attacking forces perched on the top of a wooden tower, from where she hurled imprecations and spells. For answer Hereward set fire to the tinder-dry reeds which grew everywhere in the Fens. The resulting conflagration not only consumed the witch, it drove off the attackers with many losses.

The description from the *De Gestis*, as quoted in Christina Hole's *English Folk Heroes* (London: Batsford, 1948), is worth including in full.

> Extending some two furlongs, the fire, rushing hither and thither among them, formed a horrible spectacle in the marsh, and the roar of the flames, with the cracking twigs of the brushwood and willows, made a terrible noise. Stupefied and excessively alarmed, the Normans took to flight, each man for himself; but they could not go far through the desert paths of the swamp in that watery road, nor could they keep the path with ease. Wherefore very many of them were suddenly swallowed up and overwhelmed with arrows, for in the fire and in their flight they could not with javelins resist the bands of men who came out cautiously and secretly from the Isle to repel them. And among them the woman aforesaid of infamous art in the great alarm fell down head first from her exalted position and broke her neck.

On another occasion Hereward disguised himself as a potter and having successfully penetrated the Norman camp at nearby Brandon, set fire to the woodpiles his enemies had been storing there to build a bridge across the Fens. Reputedly stopped by some soldiers as he was returning to his own camp, Hereward was asked if he knew the English leader, but replied that he did not – to his cost, since the man had stolen all his pots.

Hereward never surrendered, but after engineering an escape for himself and the majority of his men, eventually made peace with William of Normandy. His end is uncertain. One account has him falling in battle in France, where he had gone as one of the king's officers. Another refers to him dying peacefully in his bed. It seems more likely that such a brave and forthright warrior would have died in battle if at all possible, though history is, ultimately, silent on this.

His importance is summed up by Christina Hole, who gives him a fitting epitaph when she writes in her study of folk heroes:

With his submission the English resistance to the Conquest ended, and the long, slow work of welding Norman and Saxon into one nation began; but through all the changes that were to follow . . . Hereward remained and still remains a hero of the folk and one of the glowing lights of our national tradition.

Leofric of Mercia

When the weak but saintly King Edward the Confessor nominally ruled all England the land was divided into four great earldoms, of which Mercia and Kent were held by two powerful rivals. Leofric of Mercia and Godwin of Kent were jealous not only for themselves, but for their families, of each other's power and wealth, and the sons of Leofric and of Godwin were ever at strife, though the two earls were now old and prudent men, whose wars were fought with words and craft, not with swords. The wives of the two great earls were as different as their lords. The Lady Gytha, Godwin's wife, of the royal Danish race, was fierce and haughty, a fit helpmeet for the ambitious earl who was to undermine the strength of England by his efforts to win kingly power for his children. But the Lady Godiva, Leofric's beloved wife, was a gentle, pious, loving woman, who had already won an almost saintly reputation for sympathy and pity by her sacrifice to save her husband's oppressed citizens at Coventry, where her pleading won relief for them from the harsh earl on the pitiless condition of her never-forgotten ride. Happily her gentle self-suppression awoke a nobler spirit in her husband, and enabled him to play a worthier part in England's history. She was in entire sympathy with the religious aspirations of Edward the Confessor, and would gladly have seen one of her sons become a monk, perhaps to win spiritual power and a saintly reputation like those of the great Dunstan.

Hereward's Youth

For this holy vocation she fixed on her second son, Hereward, a wild, wayward lad, with long golden curls, eyes of different colours, one grey, one blue, great breadth and strength of limb, and a wild and ungovernable temper which made him difficult of control. This reckless lad the Lady Godiva vainly tried to educate for the monkish life, but he utterly refused to adopt her scheme, would not master any but the barest rudiments of learning, and spent his time in wrestling, boxing, fighting and all manly exercises. Despairing of making him an ecclesiastic, his mother set herself to inspire him with a noble ideal of knighthood, but his wildness and recklessness increased with his years, and often his mother had to stand between the riotous lad and his father's deserved anger.

His Strength and Leadership

When he reached the age of sixteen or seventeen he became the terror of the Fen Country, for at his father's Hall of Bourne he gathered a band of youths as wild and reckless as himself, who accepted him for their leader, and obeyed him implicitly, however outrageous were his commands. The wise Earl Leofric, who was much at court with the saintly king, understood little of the nature of his second son, and looked upon his wild deeds as evidence of a cruel and lawless mind, a menace to the peace of England, while they were in reality but the tokens of a restless energy for which the comparatively peaceable life of England at that time was all too dull and tame.

Leofric and Hereward

Frequent were the disputes between father and son, and sadly did Lady Godiva fore-bode an evil ending to the clash of warring nature whenever Hereward and his father met; yet she could do nothing to avert disaster, for though her entreaties would soften the lad into penitence for some mad prank or reckless outrage, one hint of cold blame from his father would suffice to make him hardened and impenitent; and so things drifted from bad to worse. In all Hereward's lawless deeds, however, there was no meanness or crafty malice. He hated monks and played many a rough trick upon them, but took his punishment, when it came, with equable cheerfulness; he robbed merchants with a high hand, but made reparation liberally, counting himself well satisfied with the fun of a fight or the skill of a clever trick; his band of youths met and fought other bands, but they bore no malice when the strife was over. In one point only was Hereward less than true to his own nobility of character – he was jealous of admitting that any man was his superior in strength or comeliness, and his vanity was well supported by his extraordinary might and beauty.

Hereward at Court

The deeds which brought Earl Leofric's wrath upon his son in a terrible fashion were not matters of wanton wickedness, but of lawless personal violence. Called to attend his father to the Confessor's court, the youth, who had little respect for one so unwarlike as 'the miracle-monger,' uttered his contempt for saintly king, Norman prelate, and studious monks too loudly, and thereby shocked the weakly devout Edward, who thought piety the whole duty of man. But his wildness touched the king more nearly still, for in his sturdy patriotism he hated the Norman favourites and courtiers who surrounded the Confessor, and again and again his marvellous strength was shown in the personal injuries he inflicted on the Normans in mere boyish brawls, until at last his father could endure the disgrace no longer.

Hereward's Exile

Begging an audience of the king, Leofric formally asked for a writ of outlawry against his own son. The Confessor, surprised, but not displeased, felt some compunction as he saw the father's affection overborne by the judge's severity. Earl Godwin, Leofric's greatest rival, was present in the council, and his pleading for the noble lad, whose faults were only those of youth, was sufficient to make Leofric more urgent in his petition. The curse of family feud, which afterwards laid England prostrate at the foot of the Conqueror, was already felt, and felt so strongly that Hereward resented Godwin's intercession more than his father's sternness.

Hereward's Farewell

'What!' he cried, 'shall a son of Leofric, the noblest man in England, accept intercession from Godwin or any of his family? No. I may be unworthy of my wise father and my saintly mother, but I am not yet sunk so low as to ask a favour from a Godwin. Father, I thank you. For years I have fretted against the peace of the land, and thus have incurred your displeasure; but in exile I may range abroad and win my fortune at the sword's point.' 'Win thy fortune, foolish boy!' said his father. 'And whither wilt thou fare?' 'Where-ever fate and my fortune lead me,' he replied recklessly. 'Perhaps to join Harald Hardrada at Constantinople and become one of the Emperor's Varangian Guard; perhaps to follow old Beowa out into the West, at the end of some day of glorious battle; perhaps to fight giants and dragons and all kinds of monsters. All these things I may do, but never shall Mercia see me again till England calls me home. Farewell, father; farewell, Earl Godwin; farewell, reverend king. I go. And pray ye that ye may never need my arm, for it may hap that ye will call me and I will not come.' Then Hereward rode away, followed into exile by one man only, Martin Lightfoot, who left the father's service for that of his outlawed son. It was when attending the king's court on this occasion that Hereward first saw and felt the charm of a lovely little Saxon maiden named Alftruda, a ward of the pious king.

Hereward in Northumbria

Though the king's writ of outlawry might run in Mercia, it did not carry more than nominal weight in Northumbria, where Earl Siward ruled almost as an independent lord. Thither Hereward determined to go, for there dwelt his own godfather, Gilbert of Ghent, and his castle was known as a good training school for young aspirants for knighthood. Sailing from Dover, Hereward landed at Whitby, and made his way to Gilbert's castle, where he was well received, since the cunning Fleming knew that an outlawry could be reversed at any time, and Leofric's son might yet come to rule England. Accordingly Hereward was enrolled in the number of young men, mainly Normans or Flemings, who were seeking to perfect themselves in chivalry before taking knighthood. He soon showed himself a brave warrior, an unequalled wrestler, and a wary fighter, and soon no one cared to meddle with the young Mercian, who outdid them all in manly sports. The envy of the young Normans was held in check by Gilbert, and by a wholesome dread of Hereward's strong arm; until, in Gilbert's absence, an incident occurred which placed the young exile on a pinnacle so far above them that only by his death could they hope to rid themselves of their feeling of inferiority.

The Fairy Bear

Gilbert kept in his castle court an immense white Polar bear, dreaded by all for its enormous strength, and called the Fairy Bear. It was even believed that the huge beast had some kinship to old Earl Siward, who bore a bear upon his crest, and was reputed to have had something of bear-like ferocity in his youth. This white bear was so much dreaded that he was kept chained up in a strong cage. One morning as Hereward was returning with Martin from his morning ride he heard shouts and shrieks from the castle yard, and, reaching the great gate, entered lightly and closed it behind him rapidly, for there outside the shattered cage, with broken chain dangling, stood the Fairy Bear, glaring savagely round the courtyard. But one human figure was in sight, that of a girl of about twelve years of age.

Hereward Slays the Bear

There were sounds of men's voices and women's shrieks from within the castle, but the doors were fast barred, while the maid, in her terror, beat on the portal with her palms, and begged them, for the love of God, to let her in. The cowards refused, and in the meantime the great bear, irritated by the dangling chain, made a rush towards the child. Hereward dashed forward, shouting to distract the bear, and just managed to stop his charge at the girl. The savage animal turned on the new-comer, who needed all his agility to escape the monster's terrible onset. Seizing his battle-axe, the youth swung it around his head and split the skull of the furious beast, which fell dead. It was a blow so mighty that even Hereward himself was surprised at its deadly effect, and approached cautiously to examine his victim. In the meantime the little girl, who proved to be no other than the king's ward, Alftruda, had watched with fascinated eyes first the approach of the monster, and then, as she crouched in terror, its sudden slaughter; and now she summoned up courage to run to Hereward, who had always been kind to the pretty child, and to fling herself into his arms. 'Kind Hereward,' she whispered, 'you have saved me and killed the bear. I love you for it, and I must give you a kiss, for my dame says so do all ladies that choose good knights to be their champions. Will you be mine?' As she spoke she kissed Hereward again and again.

Hereward's Trick on the Knights

'Where have they all gone, little one?' asked the young noble; and Alftruda replied: 'We were all out here in the courtyard watching the young men at their exercises, when we heard a crash and a roar, and the cage burst open, and we saw the dreadful Fairy Bear. They all ran, the ladies and knights, but I was the last, and they were so frightened that they shut themselves in and left me outside; and when I beat at the door and prayed them to let me in they would not, and I thought the bear would eat me, till you came.'

'The cowards!' cried Hereward. 'And they think themselves worthy of knight-hood when they will save their own lives and leave a child in danger! They must be taught a lesson. Martin, come hither and aid me.' When Martin came, the two, with infinite trouble, raised the carcase of the monstrous beast, and placed it just where the bower door, opening, would show it at once. Then Hereward bade Alftruda call to the knights in the bower that all was safe and they could come out, for the bear would not hurt them. He and Martin, listening, heard with great glee the bitter debate within the bower as to who should risk his life to open the door, the many excuses given for refusal, the mischievous fun in Alftruda's voice as she begged some one to open to her, and, best of all, the cry of horror with which the knight who had ventured to draw the bolt shut the door again on seeing the Fairy Bear waiting to enter. Hereward even carried his trick so far as to thrust the bear heavily against the bower door, making all the people within shriek and implore the protection of the saints. Finally, when he was tired of the jest, he convinced the valiant knights that they might emerge safely from their retirement, and showed how he, a stripling of seventeen, had slain the monster at one blow. From that time Hereward was the darling of the whole castle, petted, praised, beloved by all its inmates, except his jealous rivals.

Hereward Leaves Northumbria

The foreign knights grew so jealous of the Saxon youth, and so restive under his shafts of sarcastic ridicule, that they planned several times to kill him, and once or twice nearly succeeded. This insecurity, and a feeling that perhaps Earl Siward had some kinship with the Fairy Bear, and would wish to avenge his death, made Hereward decide to quit Gilbert's castle. The spirit of adventure was strong upon him, the sea seemed to call him; now that he had been acknowledged superior to the other noble youths in Gilbert's household, the castle no longer afforded a field for his ambition. Accordingly he took a sad leave of Alftruda, an affectionate one of Sir Gilbert, who wished to knight him for his brave deed, and a mocking one of his angry and unsuccessful foes.

Hereward in Cornwall

Entering into a merchant-ship, he sailed for Cornwall, and there was taken to the court of King Alef, a petty British chief, who, on true patriarchal lines, disposed of his children as he would, and had betrothed his fair daughter to a terrible Pictish giant, breaking off, in order to do it, her troth-plight with Prince Sigtryg of Waterford, son of a Danish king in Ireland. Hereward was ever chivalrous, and little Alftruda had made him feel pitiful to all maidens. Seeing speedily how the princess loathed her new betrothed, a hideous, misshapen wretch, nearly eight feet high, he determined to slay him. With great deliberation he picked a quarrel with the giant, and killed him the next day in fair fight; but King Alef was driven by the threats of the vengeful Pictish tribe to throw Hereward and his man Martin into prison, promising trial and punishment on the morrow.

Hereward Released from Prison

To the young Saxon's surprise the released princess appeared to be as grieved and as revengeful as any follower of the Pictish giant, and she not only advocated prison and death the next day, but herself superintended the tying of the thongs that bound the two strangers. When they were left to their lonely confinement Hereward began to blame the princess for hypocrisy, and to protest the impossibility of a man's ever knowing what a woman wants. 'Who would have thought,' he cried, 'that that beautiful maiden loved a giant so hideous as this Pict? Had I known, I would never have fought him, but her eyes said to me, "Kill him," and I have done so; this is how she rewards me!' 'No,' replied Martin, 'this is how'; and he cut Hereward's bonds laughing silently to himself. 'Master, you were so indignant with the lady that you could not make allowances for her. I knew that she must pretend to grieve, for her father's sake, and when she came to test our bonds I was sure of it, for as she fingered a knot she slipped a knife into my hands, and bade me use it. Now we are free from our bonds, and must try to escape from our prison.'

The Princess Visits the Captives

In vain, however, the master and man ranged round the room in which they were confined; it was a tiny chapel, with walls and doors of great thickness, and violently as Hereward exerted himself, he could make no impression on either walls or door, and, sitting sullenly down on the altar steps, he asked Martin what good was freedom from bonds in a secure prison. 'Much, every way,' replied the servant; 'at least we die with free hands; and I, for my part, am content to trust that the princess has some good plan, if we will only be ready.' While he was speaking they heard footsteps just outside the door, and the sound of a key being inserted into the lock. Hereward beckoned silently to Martin, and the two stood ready, one at each side of the door, to make a dash for freedom, and Martin was prepared to slay any who should hinder. To their great surprise, the princess entered, accompanied by an old priest bearing a lantern, which he set down on the altar step, and then the princess turned to Hereward, crying, 'Pardon me, my deliverer!' The Saxon was still aggrieved and bewildered, and replied: 'Do you now say "deliverer"? This afternoon it was "murderer, villain, cut-throat." How shall I know which is your real mind?' The princess almost laughed as she said: "How stupid men are! What could I do but pretend to hate you, since otherwise the Picts would have slain you then and us all afterwards, but I claimed you as my victims, and you have been given to me. How else could I have come here to-night? Now tell me, if I set you free will you swear to carry a message for me?'

Sigtryg Ranaldsson of Waterford

'Whither shall I go, lady, and what shall I say?' asked Hereward. 'Take this ring, my ring of betrothal, and go to Prince Sigtryg, son of King Ranald of Waterford. Say to him that I am beset on every side, and be him to come and claim me as his bride; otherwise I fear I may be forced to marry some man of my father's choosing, as I was being driven to wed the Pictish giant. From him you have rescued me, and I thank you; but if my betrothed delays his coming it may be too late, for there are other hateful suitors who would make my father bestow my hand upon one of them. Beg him to come with all speed.' 'Lady, I will go now,' said Hereward, 'if you will set me free from this vault.'

Hereward Binds the Princess

'Go quickly, and safely,' said the princess; 'but ere you go you have one duty to fulfil: you must bind me hand and foot, and fling me, with this old priest, on the ground.' 'Never,' said Hereward, 'will I bind a woman; it were foul disgrace to me for ever.' But Martin only laughed, and the maiden said again: 'How stupid men are! I must pretend to have been overpowered by you, or I shall be accused of having freed you, but I will say that I came hither to question you, and you and your man set on me and the priest, bound us, took the key, and so escaped. So shall you be free, and I shall have no blame, and my father no danger; and may Heaven forgive the lie.'

Hereward reluctantly agreed, and, with Martin's help, bound the two hand and foot and laid them before the altar; then, kissing the maiden's hand, and swearing loyalty and truth, he turned to depart. But the princess had one question to ask. 'Who are you, noble stranger, so gallant and strong? I would fain know for whom to pray.' 'I am Hereward Leofricsson, and my father is the Earl of Mercia.' 'Are you that Hereward who slew the Fairy Bear? Little wonder is it that you have slain my monster and set me free.' Then master and man left the chapel, after carefully turning the key in the lock. Making their way to the shore, they succeeded in getting a ship to carry them to Ireland, and in course of time reached Waterford.

Prince Sigtryg

The Danish kingdom of Waterford was ruled by King Ranald, whose only son, Sigtryg,was about Hereward's age, and was as noble-looking a youth as the Saxon hero. The king was at a feast, and Hereward, entering the hall with the captain of the vessel, sat down at one of the lower tables; but he was not one of those who can pass unnoticed. The prince saw him, distinguished at once his noble bearing, and asked him to come to the king's own table. He gladly obeyed, and as he drank to the prince and their goblets touched together he contrived to drop the ring from the Cornish princess into Sigtryg's cup. The prince saw and recognized it as he drained his cup, and, watching his opportunity, left the hall, and was soon followed by his guest.

Hereward and Sigtryg

Outside in the darkness Sigtryg turned hurriedly to Hereward, saying, 'You bring me a message from my betrothed?' 'Yes, if you are that Prince Sigtryg to whom the Princess of Cornwall was affianced.' 'Was affianced! What do you mean? She is still my lady and my love.' 'Yet you leave her there unaided, while her father gives her in marriage to a hideous giant of a Pict, breaking her betrothal, and driving the hapless maiden to despair. What kind of love is yours?' Hereward said nothing yet about his own slaying of the giant, because he wished to test Prince Sigtryg's sincerity, and he was satisfied, for the prince burst out: 'Would to God that I had gone to her before! but my father needed my help against foreign invaders and native rebels. I will go immediately and save my lady or die with her!' 'No need of that, for I killed that giant,' said Hereward coolly, and Sigtryg embraced him in joy and they swore blood-brotherhood together. Then he asked: 'What message do you bring me, and what means her ring?' The other replied by repeating the Cornish maiden's words, and urging him to start at once if he would save his betrothed from some other hateful marriage.

Return to Cornwall

The prince went at once to his father, told him the whole story, and obtained a ship and men to journey to Cornwall and rescue the princess; then, with Hereward by his side, he set sail, and soon landed in Cornwall, hoping to obtain his bride peaceably. To his grief he learnt that the princess had just been betrothed to a wild

Hereward and Sigtrygt

Cornish leader, Haco, and the wedding feast was to be held that very day. Sigtryg was greatly enraged, and sent a troop of forty Danes to King Alef demanding the fulfilment of the troth-plight between himself and his daughter, and threatening vengeance if it were broken. To this threat the king returned no answer, and no Dane came back to tell of their reception.

Hereward in the Enemy's Hall

Sigtryg would have waited till morning, trusting in the honour of the king, but Hereward disguised himself as a minstrel and obtained admission to the bridal feast, where he soon won applause by his beautiful singing. The bridegroom, Haco, in a rapture offered him any boon he liked to ask, but he demanded only a cup of wine from the hands of the bride. When she brought it to him he flung into the empty cup the betrothal ring, the token she had sent to Sigtryg, and said: 'I thank thee, lady, and would reward thee for thy gentleness to a wandering minstrel; I give back the cup, richer than before by the kind thoughts of which it bears the token.' The princess looked at him, gazed into the goblet, and saw her ring; then, looking again, she recognized her deliverer and knew that rescue was at hand.

Haco's Plan

While men feasted Hereward listened and talked, and found out that the forty Danes were prisoners, to be released on the morrow when Haco was sure of his bride, but released useless and miserable, since they would be turned adrift blinded. Haco was taking his lovely bride back to his own land, and Hereward saw that any rescue, to be successful, must be attempted on the march. Yet he knew not the way the bridal company would go, and he lay down to sleep in the hall, hoping that he might hear something more. When all men slept a dark shape came gliding through the hall and touched Hereward on the shoulder; he slept lightly, and awoke at once to recognize the old nurse of the princess. 'Come to her now,' the old woman whispered, and Hereward went, though he knew not that the princess was still true to her lover. In her bower, which she was soon to leave, Haco's sorrowful bride awaited the messenger.

Rescue for Haco's Bride

Sadly she smiled on the young Saxon as she said: 'I knew your face again in spite of the disguise, but you come too late. Bear my farewell to Sigtryg, and say that my father's will, not mine, makes me false to my troth-plight.' 'Have you not been told, lady, that he is here?' asked Hereward. 'Here?' the princess cried. 'I have not heard. He loves me still and has not forsaken me?' 'No, lady, he is too true a lover for falsehood. He sent forty Danes yesterday to demand you of your father and threaten his wrath if he refused.' 'And I knew not of it,' said the princess softly; 'yet I had heard that Haco had taken some prisoners, whom he means to blind.' 'Those are our messengers, and your future subjects,' said Hereward. 'Help me to save them and you. Do you know Haco's plans?' 'Only this, that he will march to-morrow along the river, and where the ravine is darkest and forms the boundary between his kingdom and my father's the prisoners are to be blinded and released.' 'Is it far hence?' 'Three miles to the eastward of this hall,' she replied. 'We will be there. Have no fear, lady, whatever you may see, but be bold and look for your lover in the fight.' So saying, Hereward kissed the hand of the princess, and passed out of the hall unperceived by any one.

The Ambush

Returning to Sigtryg, the young Saxon told all that he had learnt, and the Danes planned an ambush in the ravine where Haco had decided to blind and set free his captives. All was in readiness, and side by side Hereward and Sigtryg were watching the pathway from their covert, when the sound of horses' hoofs heard on the rocks reduced them to silence. The bridal procession came in strange array: first the Danish prisoners, bound each between two Cornishmen, then Haco and his unhappy bride, and last a great throng of Cornishmen. Hereward had taken command, that Sigtryg might look to the safety of his lady, and his plan was simplicity itself. The Danes were to wait till their comrades, with their guards, had passed through the ravine; then while the leader engaged Haco, and Sigtryg looked to the safety of the princess, the Danes would release the prisoners and slay every Cornishman, and the two parties of Danes, uniting their forces, would restore order to the land and destroy the followers of Haco.

Success

The whole was carried out exactly as Hereward had planned. The Cornishmen, with Danish captives, passed first without attack; next came Haco, riding grim and ferocious beside his silent bride, he exulting in his success, she looking eagerly for any signs of rescue. As they passed Hereward sprang from his shelter, crying, 'Upon them, Danes, and set your brethren free!' and himself struck down Haco and smote off his head. There was a short struggle, but soon the rescued Danes were able to aid their deliverers, and the Cornish guards were all slain; the men of King Alef, never very zealous for the cause of Haco, fled, and the Danes were left masters of the field. Sigtryg had in the meantime seen to the safety of the princess, and now placing her between himself and Hereward, he escorted her to the ship, which soon brought them to Waterford and a happy bridal. The Prince and Princess of Waterford always recognized in Hereward their deliverer and best friend, and in their gratitude wished him to dwell with them always; but he knew 'how hard a thing it is to look into happiness through another man's eyes,' and would not stay. His roving and daring temper drove him to deeds of arms in other lands, where he won a renown second to none, but he always felt glad in his own heart, even in later days, when unfaithfulness to a woman was the one great sin of his life, that his first feats of arms had been wrought to rescue two maidens from their hapless fate, and that he was rightly known as Hereward the Saxon, the Champion of Women.

Further Reading

'The Dream of Maxen Wiledig'

Bromwich, Rachel (trans. and ed.), *The Welsh Triads (Trioedd Ynys Prydein)*, Cardiff: University of Wales Press, 1978

Gantz: Jeffrey (trans.), *The Mabinogion*, Harmondsworth: Penguin Books, 1976

Matthews, Caitlin, *Mabon and the Mysteries of Britain: An Exploration of the Mabinogion*, London: Arkana, 1987

Matthews, Caitlin, *Arthur and the Sovereignty of Britain*, London: Arkana, 1989

'Havelok the Dane'

Bennett, J. A. W. and Smithers, G. V., *Early English Verse and Prose*, Oxford: Clarendon Press, 1966

Sands, Donald B. (ed.), *Middle English Verse Romances*, New York: Holt, Rinehart & Winston, 1966

Skeat, W. W. (ed.), rev. K. Sisam, *The Lay of Havelok the Dane*, Oxford: Clarendon Press, 1956

'Cuchulain, the Champion of Ireland'

Gregory, Lady Augusta, *Cuchulain of Muirthemne*, Gerrards Cross: Colin Smythe, 1973

Hull, Eleanor, *The Cuchullin Saga in Irish Literature*, David Nutt, 1898

Ellis, Peter Berresford, *A Dictionary of Irish Mythology*, London: Constable, 1987

O hogain, Daithi, *Myth, Legend and Romance*, London: Ryan Publishing, 1990

Stewart, Bob, *Cuchuilainn, Hound of Ulster*, Poole: Firebird Books, 1988

'The Tale of Gamelyn'

Matthews, John, *Robin Hood, Green Lord of the Wildwood*, Glastonbury: Gothic Image Publications, 1993

Sands, Donald B. (ed.), *Middle English Verse Romances*, New York: Holt, Rinehart & Winston, 1966

Skeat, W. W. (ed.), *The Tale of Gamelyn*, Oxford: Clarendon Press, 1884

'Black Colin of Loch Awe'

Moncreiffe of that Ilk, Iain, *The Highland Clans*, London: Barrie & Jenkins, 1982
Runciman, Steven, *A History of the Crusades*, Cambridge: Cambridge University Press, 3 vols, 1951–4

'The Marriage of Sir Gawain'

Brian Stone (ed.), *Gawain and the Green Knight*, Harmondsworth: Penguin Books, 1976
Madden, Frederic, *Syr Gawain*, New York: AMS Press, 1971
Matthews, Caitlin and John, *The Ladies of the Lake*, London: Thorsons, 1992
Matthews, John, *Gawain, Knight of the Goddess*, London: Thorsons, 1991
Percy, Bishop, *Reliques of Ancient English Poetry* (1857), reprinted in Stewart, R. J., *Celtic Gods, Celtic Goddesses*, London: Blandford Press, 1994
Sands, Donald B. (ed.), *Middle English Verse Romances*, New York: Holt, Rinehart & Winston, 1966
Whiting, B. J. in Bryan, W. F. and Dempster, G., *Sources and Analogues of Chaucer's Canterbury Tales*, London: Routledge, 1958

'King Horn'

French, Walter H., *Essays on King Horn*, Ithaca, NY: Cornell University Press, 1940
Crossley Holland, Kevin, *King Horn: A Medieval Romance*, London: Macmillan, 1965
Sands, Donald B. (ed.), *Medieval English Verse Romances*, New York: Holt, Rinehart & Winston, 1966
Spiers, John, *Medieval English Poetry*, London: Faber, 1971
Wells, Joseph (ed.), *King Horn*, Oxford: Clarendon Press, 1901

'Robin Hood'

Clawson, W. H., *The Gest of Robin Hood*, Toronto: University of Toronto Press, 1909
Holt, J. C., *Robin Hood*, London: Thames & Hudson, 1983
Matthews, John, *Robin Hood: Green Lord of the Wildwood*, Glastonbury: Gothic Image Publications, 1993

'Hereward the Wake'

Earle, J. and Plummer, C. (eds), *Two of the Saxon Chronicles*, Oxford: Clarendon Press, 2 vols, 1892–9
Hole, Christina, *English Folk Heroes*, London: Batsford, 1948
Sutcliff, Rosemary: *Heroes and History*, London: Batsford, 1965

Index

Abbot of St Mary's Abbey 125, 127–9
Ablac, *see* Havelok the Dane
Ailill, King of Connaught 41–5
Ailmar, King of Westernesse 102–7, 109, 112, 114, 116–17
Alef, King 141, 146, 147
Alftruda 139, 140, 141
Anglesey (Mona), Isle of 17
Anglo-Saxon Chronicle 134–5
Argyll 69
Armagh 39, 40, 42, 43, 45
Arnoldin, Sir 117
Arthur, King 4, 5–6, 7, 8, 98
    marriage of Sir Gawain 83, 85–94, 97
As You Like It (Shakespeare) 52
Athelbrus, Sir 103–6, 117
Athelny 7
Athelstan, King of England 20
Athelwold, King 25–7
Athulf, Sir 101–2, 104, 106–7, 109, 112–17
Avalon 6

Banier, Sir 85, 92
Barbour, John 69–70
Barnsdale 119, 121, 129
Barton, Andrew 68
'Battle of Bannockburn, The' (Barbour) 69–70
Bedivere, Sir 85
Bedrugan Head 7
'Beheading Game' 37
Beli (son of Manogan) 19
Bell, Adam 75
Beowa 139
Berild, Prince 11

Birkabeyn, King 23, 30, 32, 33
Black Colin of Loch Awe, *see* Colin of Loch Awe
Black Monk 131–2
Book of the Dun Cow 37
Bors, Sir 7, 85, 92
Bosworth, Battle of 7
Boudicca, Queen 2
Bourne 134
Bourne Hall 137
Boyne River 7
Bran the Blessed 6
Brandon 135
Bricriu of the Bitter Tongue 37–8, 39–41
Brown, Bernard 30–2
Byron, George Gordon, Lord 2

Caer Seint 12
Caerlleon Castle 19
Caermarthen Castle 19
Caernarvon (Segontium) 12, 17, 19
Campbell clan 68–9, 72, 73
Campbell, Sir Colin 69
Campbell, Sir Nigel 71
Canterbury Tales, The (Chaucer) 53
Carlisle 85, 86, 88, 91, 94
Caswallawn (Cassivellaunus), King 14
Cathbad the Druid 39
'Cattle Raid of Cooley' 37
Celtic Myth and Legend: Poetry and Romance (Squire) 1
Chambers, E.K. 7
'Charge of the Light Brigade' (Tennyson) 2

Chaucer, Geoffrey 53, 82
Chesterton, G.K. 8
Chronicle (Langtoft) 21
Cole of Colchester (Old King Cole) 12
Colin of Loch Awe 4, 7, 68–81
    leaves for the Crusades 71–3
    return to Glenurchy 76–81
Conall Cearnach 40–5, 48–9
Connacht 37
Conor, King of Ulster 39, 41, 42, 43, 45, 49
Constantine III, King of Scotland 20
Constantine the Great, Emperor 12, 19
Constantius Chlorus 12
Cornwall 141, 144–5
Coventry 137
Cruachan 42, 43, 45
Crusades 69, 71–2, 73–4, 125
Cuchulain, Champion of Ireland 7, 8, 36–51
    Bricriu's feast 39–41
    at Connaught 42–5
    marriage 39
    slays the dragon 45–7
    and Uath the Stranger 48–51
    youth 39
Curoi of Kerry 45, 46–8, 51
Cuthbert, *see* Horn, King

De Gestis Herwardi 134, 135
Dechtire (daughter of Cathbad) 36, 39

'Destruction of Sennacherib, The' (Byron) 2
Diarmuid-Siol 69
Dinas Bran 6
Dindsenchas, The 6
Domesday Book 134
Dover 27, 139
Duncan mac Duibhne, Chieftain 69
Dunstan 137

Ebbutt, M.I. 2, 8–9, 11, 20, 68, 83
Edinburgh 73
Edward I, King of England 54, 67, 71, 125
Edward II, King of England 71
Edward the Confessor, King 137, 138
Edwin, Prince 134
Elen (Princess Helena) 11–12, 17–19
Elizabeth I, Queen of England 2
Emain Macha 7
Emer (daughter of Forgall the Wily) 36–7, 39, 41, 44
English Folk Heroes (Hole) 5, 135–6
English Folk-Play (Chambers) 7
Ercol 44
Estoires des Engles 21
Eudav (son of Caradoc) 19
Excalibur 86, 8

Fairy Bear 139–40, 141
Fedelm 41
Fernandyne 52
Fikenhild 101, 107–8, 116, 117
Finn (Scottish hero) 68
First World War 2
Fled Bricriu 37
Forgall the Wily 39
Frazer, Sir George 3
Friar Tuck 119, 123

Gaimer, Geoffrey 21
Gamelyn 52–67
  arrest 65
  attacks the churchmen 61–3
  chained by Sir John 60
  fight with Sir John's servants 55–7
  joins the outlaws 64
  releases Otho 66–7
  the wrestling match 57–9
Gareth, Sir 85, 92–3

'Gawain and the Green Knight' 37, 83
Gawain, Sir 82, 85, 92–7
Gest of Robin Hood' 119
Gilbert of Ghent 139, 141
Glenurchy 71, 74, 76, 81
Godard, Jarl 23–5, 30, 33–4
Godhild, Queen of Suddene 101
Godiva, Lady 134, 137, 138
Godrich, Earl of Cornwall 27, 28–9, 34–5
Godwin of Kent 137, 138–9
Goldborough, Princess 25–33
Golden Bough, The (Frazer) 3
Gothfrithson, Olaf 20
Gratian, Emperor 11
Great War 2
Green Knight (Gromer Somer Jour) 83
Green Man 119
Gregory, Lay Augusta 37
Griffin the Welshman 32
Grim the fisherman 21, 24–5, 27, 29
Grimsby 7, 21, 29
Gromer Somer Jour (Green Knight) 83
Guenever, Queen 85, 86, 91, 94, 95, 97
Guest, Lady Charlotte 11, 14
Guinglain (son of Sir Gawain) 83
Gwalchmai *see* Gawain, Sir
Gytha, Lady 137

Haco of Cornwall 146–7
Hamlet (Shakespeare) 98
Harald Hardrada 139
Harold, Prince 111
Havelok the Dane 7, 20–35, 52, 98
  as cook's boy 27–8
  death of Godard 33–4
  death of Godrich 34–5
  marries Princess Goldborough 28–9
  return to Denmark 29–30
  and Ubbe 30–3
Helena (Elen), Princess 11–12, 17–19
Henry of Bedrugan 7
Heraclitus 7
Hereward the Wake 4, 7, 134–47
  in Cornwall 141
  defeat of Haco 146–7
  exile 138–9

and the Fairy Bear 139–40
  imprisonment 141–3
  in Northumbria 139
  return to Cornwall 144–6
  in Waterford 143–4
Hero, The (Lord Raglan) 3–4
Herod, King 98
Heroes and History (Sutcliffe) 3
Hole, Christina 5, 135–6
Hood, Robin 4, 5, 6, 7, 52, 53, 118–33
  capture of the Black Monk 131–2
  meets Sir Richard of the Lea 123–6, 133
Hope Moncrieff, A.R. 1
'Horatius' (Macaulay) 2
Horn, King 20, 52, 98–117
  arrives at Westernesse 102
  banishment 109
  cast adrift by Saracens 101–2
  at court in Westernesse 103–6
  in Ireland 109–11
  kills Fikenhild 117
  kills Giant Emir 111
  kills King Modi 114
  kills Saracen leader 107–8
  knighted 106
  return to Westernesse 112–14
  returns to Suddene 115–16
Hugh the Raven 30, 32
'Hynd Horn' 99–100

Innis Eoalan 76
Innischonaill Castle 69
Inveraray 69
Iseult White Hands 99
Isle of Ely 7, 134, 135

Jerusalem 73, 76
Joan of Arc 2
John of the Marches, Sir 54–5
John the Younger, Sir 54–67

Kay, Sir 85, 92, 93, 94, 97
Kent 137
Kerry 45
Kilchurn Castle 80–1
'King Horn' *see* Horn, King

Laegaire 37, 40, 42–5, 48–9
Lancelot, Sir 85, 92
Langtoft, Peter, *Chronicle* 21
Lay of Havelok 20, 21
Le Fay, Morgan 83
Leith 73

Lendabair the Favourite 41
Leofric of Mercia, Earl 134,
    137–8
Leve, Dame 25
Life of Hereward the Saxon 134
Lightfoot, Martin 139, 140,
    141, 143
Lincoln 27, 28, 34
Little John 119, 121–32
Loch Awe 7, 69
Loch Fine 69
Lodge, Thomas 52
Lugh of the Long hand (Lugh
    Lamhfada) 36, 39

Mabinogian, The 8, 11, 14
Macaulay, Thomas
    Babbington, Lord 2
MacCorquodale, Baron Niel
    73–7, 80–1
McCumhail, Fionn 36
MacGregor clan 71, 76
'Madness of Tristan' 99
Magnus Clemens Maximus
    (Maxen Wledig), Emperor
    4, 11–19
Maid Marian 119
Manning, Robert 21
Maxen Wledig (Magnus
    Clemens Maximus),
    Emperor 4, 11–19
Meath 7
Meave, Queen of Connaught
    41–5
Medieval English Poetry (Spiers)
    100
Mercia 137, 139
Modi, King of Reynes 112,
    113, 114, 117
Mona (Anglesey), Isle of
    17
Moncreiffe, Sir Iain 69
Morcar, Prince 134
Mordred, Sir 85
Morrigan, The 37, 83
Much the miller's son 119,
    121, 126, 131
Murry, King of Suddene 101,
    107, 111, 112, 115
'Myth of Àrthur, The'
    (Chesterton) 8
*Myths and Legends of the Celtic
    Race* (Rolleston) 1

Nine Christian Worthies 8
Northumbria 139

o'Duibhne, Diarmuid 69
Oisin (Scottish hero) 68

Old King Cole 12
Orchy, River 71
Otho 54, 65–7

Paladins of Charlemagne 8
Patterson family 71, 76, 77–9
Pendragon Castle 6
Percy, Bishop 83–4
Peterborough 134
Picts 141, 143
Plain of Mag Murcraime 7

Raglan, Lord, *The Hero* 3–4
Ragnall 82, 83
Ranald of Waterford, King
    143, 144
'Red Branch Heroes' 37, 39,
    42–3, 48–51
Reliques of Ancient English Poetry
    (Percy) 83–4
Reynild, Princess 99, 111, 117
Rhodes 73
Richard of the Leas, Sir
    123–31
Robert the Bruce, King 68, 69,
    71
Robert the Red 30, 33
'Robin and Gandelyn' 53
'Robin Hood Newly Arrived'
    53
Rolleston, T.W. 1
Romance and Legend of Chivalry
    (Hope Moncrieff) 1
Rome 73
Rosader 52
*Rosalynde, or Euphues' Golden
    Legacy* (Lodge) 52
Rymenhild, Princess 98–100,
    104–17

Saladyne 52
Saracens 98, 101, 107, 108,
    111, 116
Sarnau Elen (Elen's Roads) 12,
    19
Saxons 5
Scarlet, Will 53, 119, 121,
    131
Scathach 37
Scottish national heroes 68
Segontium (Caernarvon) 12,
    17, 19
Setanta, *see* Cuchulain,
    Champion of Ireland
Shakespeare, William 52, 98
Shannon, River 7
Sherwood Forest 121
Sigtryg of Waterford, Prince
    141, 143–7

Sigtryggson, Olaf, King 20
'Sir Gawain and the Green
    Knight' 37, 83
Siward of Northumbria, Earl
    139, 141
Socach 71
Spencer, Adam 60–1, 63–4,
    66, 67
Spiers, John, *Medieval English
    Poetry* 100
Squire, Charles, *Celtic Myth and
    Legend: Poetry and Romance* 1
Stephen, Sir 92
Suddene 98, 101, 103, 115,
    116, 117
Sutcliffe, Rosemary 3

'Tain, The' 37
'Tales of the Red Branch
    Heroes' 8
Tarn Wathelan Castle 86, 88,
    89, 92, 96–7
Tennyson, Alfred, Lord 2
Theodosius, Emperor 11
Thurston, King of Ireland 111,
    112
Triads 14
Tristan 7, 99
Tuck, Friar 119, 123
Turold, Abbot 134

Uath the Stranger 48–51
Ubbe, Jarl 30–5
Ulster 37, 38, 39
Uterysdale 133
Uther Pendragon 6

Varangian, Emperor 139
Vikings 98

Wallace, William 68, 71
Waterford 141, 143, 144,
    147
Watling Street 131
Wayland Wood (Norfolk) 6
Wendut, William 30
Westernesse 98, 102, 103,
    112, 116, 117
Whitby 139
'Wicked Elder Brothers' 52
'Wife of Bath's Tale' 82
Will Scarlet 53, 119, 121,
    131
William I (William the
    Conqueror), King of
    England 5, 135, 138
Winchester 27

'Yeoman's Tale' 53
York 125, 127